P9-DUE-459

Sunset

Fresh Ways with
Salads

By the Editors of Sunset Books
and Sunset Magazine

Enjoy garden-fresh flavor in
Romaine Salad with Creamy Garlic Dressing (page 5)

Lane Publishing Co. ■ Menlo Park, California

The Contemporary Salad

In an age fascinated by both fitness and good food, salad has naturally come into its own. No longer a quiet plate of greens, salad today has become an adventure that greets your palate with everything from radicchio curls to cactus pads. Even its appearance has changed—instead of simply being tossed together, salads are often as carefully composed as a work of art.

As a glance through the pages of this book will reveal, the contemporary salad is anything but predictable. It appears as the main course at lunch or dinner, as a substantial side dish using pasta or rice, as a showy fruit dessert, and even as a make-ahead molded creation. Whatever the occasion, salads have never before offered so much in so many versatile, fresh-tasting, and surprising ways.

For our recipes, we provide a nutritional analysis prepared by Hill Nutrition Associates, Inc., of New York. Generally, the nutritional information applies to a single serving, based on the largest number of servings given for each recipe. The analysis does not include optional ingredients or those for which no specific amount is stated. If an ingredient is listed with an option or a range is given for the amount, the information was calculated using the first choice.

For their generosity in sharing props for use in our photographs, we're grateful to The Abacus, Best of All Worlds, Crate & Barrel, Menlo Park Hardware, Taylor & Ng, and Williams-Sonoma.

Research & Text
Cynthia Scheer

Contributing Editor
Karen Hewitt

Coordinating Editor
Suzanne Normand Mathison

Design
Kathy Avanzino Barone

Illustrations
Rik Olson

Photo Stylist
JoAnn Masaoka

Photographers
Glenn Christiansen, pages 10, 89; **Michael Lamotte,** page 45; **Darrow M. Watt,** pages 24, 25, 44, 71, 72, 73, 87; **Tom Wyatt,** page 59; **Nikolay Zurek,** pages 1, 2, 7, 8, 9, 15, 16, 17, 18, 23, 26, 31, 35, 36, 37, 38, 43, 46, 51, 52, 53, 54, 60, 61, 62, 65, 66, 74, 79, 80, 81, 82, 88, 90, 95, 96

Cover: Salad artistry finds expression in Strawberry Chicken Salad Plates (page 41), an attractive—and nutritious—combination of tender breast meat and fresh fruit. Design by Sandra Popovich. Photograph by Nikolay Zurek. Photo styling by JoAnn Masaoka. Food styling by Cynthia Scheer.

Sunset Books
   Editor: David E. Clark
   Managing Editor: Elizabeth L. Hogan

Second printing July 1987

Copyright © 1987, 1979, 1966, 1962, 1937, Lane Publishing Co., Menlo Park, CA 94025. Fifth edition. World rights reserved. No part of this publication may be reproduced by any mechanical, photographic, or electronic process, or in the form of a phonographic recording, nor may it be stored in a retrieval system, transmitted, or otherwise copied for public or private use without prior written permission from the publisher. Library of Congress Catalog Card Number: 86-82778. ISBN 0-376-02608-1. Lithographed in the United States.

Parmesan cheese and anchovies lend traditional flavor to Caesar Salad (page 5)

CONTENTS

SPECIAL FEATURES

Green & Vegetable Salads

Crisp and fresh, green salads can be the perfect start, finish, or accent to any meal. The variety of salad greens now available in markets is greater than ever before, and the recipes in this chapter take full advantage of the diversity. From the classic Caesar Salad with romaine to the very contemporary Radicchio with Butter Lettuce, there's a salad for every taste.

You'll find, too, that the look of salads has changed. Not every salad is just "tossed together." Many are strikingly beautiful compositions that are easy to assemble.

Vegetables take on a new dimension when served as salads. Zucchini-Apple Slaw and Leeks in Creamy Tarragon Dressing are just two of the many possibilities.

Caesar Salad

Classic Caesar salad is a favorite dating back several generations. Carry on the tradition with this tempting version. *(Pictured on page 2.)*

1 small clove garlic, minced or pressed
⅓ cup olive oil or salad oil
1 cup croutons, purchased or homemade (see page 55)
1 large head romaine lettuce, washed and crisped
   Salt and pepper
1 egg
2 tablespoons lemon juice
3 to 4 anchovy fillets, drained well and chopped
¼ cup grated Parmesan cheese

Combine garlic and oil and, if time permits, let stand for several hours. Heat 2 tablespoons of the garlic-flavored oil in a frying pan over medium heat. Add croutons and stir often until browned; set aside.

Tear lettuce into bite-size pieces (you should have about 3 quarts). Place lettuce in a salad bowl and season with salt and pepper to taste. Pour remaining garlic-flavored oil over lettuce and mix lightly until well coated. Slip egg into boiling water for 1 minute; remove and break over salad. Drizzle lemon juice over all and mix thoroughly. Add anchovies and cheese; mix lightly but thoroughly. Add croutons and mix lightly again. Serve immediately. Makes 6 servings.

Per serving: 315 calories, 10 grams protein, 29 grams carbohydrates, 18 grams total fat, 50 milligrams cholesterol, 447 milligrams sodium.

Romaine Salad with Creamy Garlic Dressing

The bold garlic flavor of our creamy dressing accents crisp lettuce, juicy tomatoes, and mellow avocado in a tantalizing summer salad. *(Pictured on page 1.)*

2 cloves garlic, minced or pressed
½ teaspoon salt
1 tablespoon lime or lemon juice
1 egg
⅓ cup mayonnaise
2 teaspoons Worcestershire or soy sauce
1 medium-size ripe avocado

1 large head romaine lettuce, washed and crisped
3 tablespoons grated Parmesan cheese
1 cup cherry tomatoes, halved
2 green onions, thinly sliced
⅔ cup seasoned croutons, purchased or homemade (page 55)

Combine garlic and salt; mash into a paste with back of a spoon or use a mortar and pestle. Stir in lime juice; add egg and beat until foamy. Stir in mayonnaise and Worcestershire. If made ahead, cover and refrigerate for up to 1 week.

Just before serving, pit, peel, and dice avocado. Tear lettuce into bite-size pieces (you should have about 3 quarts). In a salad bowl, combine lettuce, avocado, cheese, tomatoes, onions, and croutons. Stir dressing until well blended; pour over salad and mix lightly until well coated. Serve immediately. Makes 6 to 8 servings.

Per serving: 170 calories, 4 grams protein, 8 grams carbohydrates, 14 grams total fat, 41 milligrams cholesterol, 315 milligrams sodium.

Provençal Mixed Green Salad

Popular in the south of France, a lively green salad called *mesclun* combines spirited young arugula, butter lettuce, and dandelion leaves. Our own mix of assertive greens differs slightly, yet captures the classic flavor.

5 tablespoons olive oil
1½ tablespoons cider vinegar
1½ teaspoons Dijon mustard
3 tablespoons minced fresh chervil or parsley
1 cup lightly packed bite-size pieces arugula (rocket) or watercress leaves, washed and crisped
2 cups lightly packed bite-size pieces butter lettuce or Belgian endive, washed and crisped
3 cups lightly packed bite-size pieces chicory, washed and crisped
   Salt and pepper

In a salad bowl, combine oil, vinegar, mustard, and chervil; mix until well blended. Add greens and mix lightly until well coated. Season with salt and pepper to taste. Serve immediately. Makes 4 servings.

Per serving: 185 calories, 2 grams protein, 6 grams carbohydrates, 18 grams total fat, 0 milligram cholesterol, 380 milligrams sodium.

SALAD GREENS: THE BASICS

Each season brings a new harvest of crisp greens to tempt salad lovers. Many of the newer varieties have a pronounced zestiness that may be too intense if used alone. But paired with a milder green, they add intriguing flavor. As you grow accustomed to their pleasant bite, try recipes specifically developed for these tasty greens.

The selection of fresh salad greens described below and shown at right indicates the rich variety that awaits you in markets today. For information on how to handle salad greens, see page 12.

Arugula (rocket, roquette). Arugula is a tender, spicy, mustardy-flavored green. Some varieties have smooth-edged leaves; others have serrated leaves.

Baby bok choy. Harvested young, baby bok choy is a milder-flavored version of the mature green, which has a cabbagelike taste.

Baby chicory (frisée). More softly textured than mature chicory, baby chicory has a subtly bitter flavor.

Belgian endive (French endive, Witloof chicory). The slender, firm leaves of Belgian endive are creamy white with pale yellow tips; their flavor is distinctive and pleasantly bitter.

Butter lettuce. Notably delicate and ruffled, the leaves of butter lettuce taste faintly buttery.

Chicory (curly endive). Chicory's coarse dark green leaves are crisp and pleasantly bitter.

Escarole. A sturdy, broad-leafed variety of endive, escarole has a pronounced, mildly bitter flavor.

Green cabbage. So pale that it's sometimes called white cabbage, green cabbage has a firm, compact head and a distinctive flavor.

Green leaf lettuce. A variety of looseleaf lettuce, green leaf is a relatively crisp lettuce that's tender and delicately flavored.

Iceberg lettuce (crisphead). The perennial best-seller because of its dependably crisp texture and mild flavor, iceberg lettuce is being put to new uses as a cooling palate refresher for fiery hot dishes.

Limestone lettuce. A form of butterhead lettuce, limestone lettuce has delicate leaves that are at once soft and crisp.

Napa cabbage (celery cabbage, Chinese cabbage). A bit sweeter than more familiar cabbages, napa cabbage has a moist crispness and a slightly zesty flavor.

Radicchio (red chicory, Italian red lettuce). Small, round, or elongated heads of radicchio taste somewhat like escarole; the sturdy leaves range from purplish red to variegated red and green.

Red cabbage. Similar in form and flavor to the green variety, red cabbage has royal purple leaves.

Red leaf lettuce. A colorful salad green, red leaf lettuce is known for its mild-flavored red to bronze-tinged leaves.

Red oak-leaf lettuce. Most of the leaves of this tender and mild-tasting lettuce are so small you can use them whole.

Romaine lettuce (Cos). Romaine lettuce is a favorite for its mild flavor and lasting crunchiness.

Spinach. Some varieties of spinach have smooth-textured leaves; others are more crinkled. Served raw, both types have an earthy, lemony taste.

Watercress. Often used as a garnish and increasingly featured as a salad green, watercress is noted for its peppery flavor. ■

Watercress

Red oak-leaf lettuce

Napa cabbage

Iceberg lettuce

Belgian endive

Baby bok choy

Radicchio

Baby chicory

Arugula

Green leaf lettuce

Limestone lettuce

Red leaf lettuce

Butter lettuce

Romaine lettuce

Spinach

Escarole

Green cabbage

Red cabbage

Chicory

Salad Italiano with Basil Dressing

Basil, a favorite herb of Italian cuisine, brightens the dressing of this tossed green salad with Mediterranean flavor.

Combine cheese, vinegar, mustard, salt, pepper, oil, onions, and basil. Mix until well blended; set aside. (Basil will darken if dressing is made more than 2 hours ahead.)

Peel and thinly slice cucumber; cut tomatoes into thin wedges. In a salad bowl, layer greens, cucumber, and garbanzos; arrange tomatoes on top. (At this point, you may cover and refrigerate for up to 2 hours.) Mix dressing again until well blended; pour over salad and mix lightly until well coated. Sprinkle with croutons and serve immediately. Makes 6 to 8 servings.

Per serving: 210 calories, 5 grams protein, 19 grams carbohydrates, 13 grams total fat, 1 milligram cholesterol, 328 milligrams sodium.

Salad Italiano with Basil Dressing

The colors and aromas of Italy come alive at your table with this fresh summertime salad, made bold by a basil-and-Parmesan dressing.

> 3 tablespoons *each* grated Parmesan cheese and red wine vinegar
> ½ teaspoon dry mustard
> ¼ teaspoon *each* salt and pepper
> 6 tablespoons olive oil or salad oil
> ¼ cup chopped green onions
> ½ cup lightly packed fresh basil leaves, chopped
> 1 small cucumber
> 2 small tomatoes
> 3 quarts lightly packed bite-size pieces mixed salad greens, washed and crisped
> 1 can (8 oz.) garbanzos, drained
> ½ cup croutons, purchased or homemade (page 55)

Radicchio with Butter Lettuce

The rosy radicchio in this elegant salad catches the eye immediately. But just as impressive—to the palate—is the hot bacon dressing.

> 3 slices bacon
> Salad oil (optional)
> 1 tablespoon *each* red wine vinegar and minced shallots
> ½ teaspoon Dijon mustard
> 1 medium-size orange
> 2 cups lightly packed coarsely torn or small butter lettuce leaves, washed and crisped
> 3 cups lightly packed radicchio leaves, washed and crisped
> Salt and pepper
> Whole chives or long slivers of green onion tops (optional)

In a wide frying pan, cook bacon over medium heat until crisp. Lift out, reserving drippings; drain and break into 1-inch pieces.

Radicchio with Butter Lettuce

In this alternative to the traditional green dinner salad, delicate butter lettuce and segments of sweet orange temper the distinctive bite of radicchio.

Measure drippings and add enough salad oil, if necessary, to make 3 tablespoons. Return drippings to pan with bacon, vinegar, shallots, and mustard. (At this point, you may cover and refrigerate until next day.)

Cut off peel and white membrane from orange; cut between inner membranes, removing orange segments. In a large bowl, combine lettuce, radicchio, and orange segments. Heat bacon mixture to simmering over medium heat. Immediately pour hot dressing over salad and mix quickly until well coated. Season with salt and pepper to taste.

Arrange salad on individual plates. Garnish, if desired, with a spray of chives radiating out from salad. Serve immediately. Makes 4 servings.

Per serving: 133 calories, 3 grams protein, 7 grams carbohydrates, 11 grams total fat, 9 milligrams cholesterol, 133 milligrams sodium.

Gorgonzola, Apple & Walnut Salad

Fruit, nuts, and cheese form a classic trio of flavors. Here, they're combined with crisp lettuce in an imaginative salad perfect for an autumn dinner party.

Gingered Walnuts (recipe follows)
¼ **cup** *each* **walnut oil and salad oil**
2 **tablespoons** *each* **white wine vinegar and lemon juice**
2 **teaspoons Dijon mustard**
⅛ **teaspoon salt**
 Dash of white pepper
2 **large tart green apples**
1 **large head romaine or green leaf lettuce, washed and crisped**
3 **ounces (about ⅔ cup) crumbled Gorgonzola or other blue-veined cheese**

Prepare Gingered Walnuts and set aside. In a medium-size bowl, combine oils, vinegar, lemon juice, mustard, salt, and pepper; mix until well blended. Set aside.

Just before serving, core and thinly slice apples. Tear lettuce into bite-size pieces (you should have about 3 quarts). In a salad bowl, combine lettuce and apples. Mix dressing again; pour over salad and mix lightly until well coated. Sprinkle salad with walnuts and cheese. Serve immediately. Makes 6 to 8 servings.

Gingered Walnuts. Pour 1 tablespoon **salad oil** into an 8-inch square baking pan. Place pan in oven; preheat to 250°. When oven is hot, remove pan and stir in 1 teaspoon **soy sauce,** ¼ teaspoon *each* **ground ginger** and **salt,** and ⅛ teaspoon **garlic powder.** Add 1 cup **walnut halves,** stirring to coat with oil mixture. Spread nuts in a single layer. Bake, stirring occasionally, until nuts are crisp and browned (about 30 minutes). Let cool on paper towels. If made ahead, store nuts in an airtight container at room temperature for up to 1 week. Makes about 1 cup.

Per serving: 290 calories, 6 grams protein, 10 grams carbohydrates, 27 grams total fat, 8 milligrams cholesterol, 352 milligrams sodium.

Spinach Salad with Crisp Red Chiles

Lively with Latin flavors, this dish from Mexico City offers a piquant variation on the standard spinach salad. Dot it with mild white cheese and serve as a light lunch or as an accompaniment to barbecued meat or chicken.

> 6 **large dried Anaheim chiles**
> ¼ **cup olive oil or salad oil**
> 1 **pound fresh whole or diced cactus (nopales) or 1½ cups canned diced cactus (nopalitos), drained**
> 1 **pound spinach, washed and crisped**
> ¼ **pound watercress, washed and crisped**
> 1 **large red onion, thinly sliced**
> 1 **cup sliced radishes**
> 1 **pound queso asadero or mozzarella cheese, cut into ½-inch cubes**
> 2 **large ripe avocados**
> **Cider Dressing (recipe follows)**

Wipe chiles clean with a damp towel. With scissors, cut chiles into thin, crosswise strips; discard seeds and stems. In a wide frying pan, combine oil and chiles. Cook, stirring, over low heat until chiles are crisp (2 to 3 minutes); watch closely to avoid burning. Lift out chiles and set aside; reserve oil for dressing.

If using fresh cactus, hold cactus pad with tongs and use a knife to scrape off any spines or prickly hairs (wear gloves to protect your hands). Trim around edge of pad to remove skin; then peel remaining pad if skin is tough. Cut cactus into about ½-inch squares.

In a 3- to 4-quart pan, bring about 2 quarts water to a boil. Add fresh cactus and simmer, uncovered, until cactus is barely tender when pierced (about 5 minutes). Drain and rinse well to remove any mucilaginous coating. Do *not* cook canned cactus.

Remove and discard coarse spinach and watercress stems. Tear spinach into bite-size pieces (you should have about 4 quarts). Place half the spinach in a salad bowl. Top with half *each* of the watercress, cactus, onion, radishes, and cheese. Repeat layers.

Spinach Salad with Crisp Red Chiles

Discover a world of new flavors in a familiar salad. Here, watercress, nopales, chiles, and queso asadero mix with tender spinach.

(At this point, you may cover and refrigerate for up to 4 hours.)

Just before serving, pit, peel, and slice avocados. Arrange avocado slices and chiles over salad. Prepare Cider Dressing; pour over salad and mix lightly until well coated. Serve immediately. Makes 6 to 8 servings.

Cider Dressing. Combine ⅔ cup **cider vinegar;** reserved **oil** from chiles; 1 clove **garlic,** minced or pressed; 1 tablespoon **soy sauce;** and ¼ teaspoon **pepper.** Mix until well blended.

Per serving: 362 calories, 15 grams protein, 14 grams carbohydrates, 29 grams total fat, 44 milligrams cholesterol, 439 milligrams sodium.

Green & Orange Salad

Fresh citrus flavor infuses this leafy salad with zest that's especially welcome in winter. There's orange juice in the dressing and orange segments in the salad.

> 2 **large, juicy oranges**
> ⅔ **cup salad oil**
> 3 **tablespoons white wine vinegar**
> 1 **teaspoon *each* salt and dry mustard**
> 4 **teaspoons sugar**
> **Dash of white pepper**
> 1 **large head butter lettuce, washed and crisped**
> 1 **small head romaine lettuce, washed and crisped**
> 1 **small cucumber, thinly sliced**
> 3 **green onions, thinly sliced**

Grate enough peel from oranges to make 1 tablespoon; reserve for dressing. Cut off peel and white membrane from oranges. Holding oranges over a bowl to collect juices, cut between inner membranes, removing orange segments.

In a medium-size bowl, combine oil, vinegar, salt, mustard, sugar, pepper, reserved orange peel, and 2 tablespoons of the orange juice (if there is not enough juice, squeeze another orange). Mix until well blended; set aside.

Tear lettuce into bite-size pieces (you should have about 3½ quarts). In a salad bowl, combine lettuce, cucumber, onions, and orange segments. Mix dressing again; pour over salad and mix lightly until well coated. Serve immediately. Makes 6 to 8 servings.

Per serving: 210 calories, 2 grams protein, 11 grams carbohydrates, 19 grams total fat, 0 milligram cholesterol, 283 milligrams sodium.

HOW TO WASH & CRISP SALAD GREENS

Salad greens bruise easily, so handle them gently at every stage of preparation.

Core iceberg and other tight-head lettuces; then hold the head under cold running water, carefully separating the leaves. To wash looseleaf lettuces, endive, and spinach, separate the leaves and plunge them into a large quantity of cold water so that dirt will float free (rinse several times if necessary). Wash watercress by the bunch in several changes of water.

Shake off or drain away as much water as possible; discard any bruised leaves. Dry the greens with paper towels or clean kitchen towels, or whirl them in a salad spinner. Then wrap them loosely in paper towels, place them in a plastic bag, and refrigerate for at least 30 minutes or until chilled and crisp.

Most greens will keep in the refrigerator for 2 days; iceberg and romaine lettuce will keep for up to 5 days.

Spinach-Cauliflower Toss

A study in contrasts, this crisp salad will brighten any winter buffet. A special bonus is that it doesn't wilt as readily as other salads do. *(Pictured on page 96.)*

½ **cup pine nuts or slivered almonds**
½ **pound spinach, washed and crisped**
2 **cups cauliflower flowerets (about ½ medium-size head)**
1 **large ripe avocado**
    Lemon juice
6 **tablespoons salad oil**
3 **tablespoons white wine vinegar**
1 **large clove garlic, minced or pressed**
½ **teaspoon *each* salt, dry mustard, and dry basil**
¼ **teaspoon pepper**
    Dash of ground nutmeg

In a small frying pan, toast nuts over medium heat, shaking pan often, until nuts are golden (3 to 5 minutes). Set aside.

Remove and discard coarse spinach stems. Tear larger leaves into bite-size pieces. Slice cauliflower pieces ¼ inch thick. Pit, peel, and slice avocado; dip slices in lemon juice to coat. Combine with spinach and cauliflower in a salad bowl.

In a small bowl, combine oil, vinegar, garlic, salt, mustard, basil, pepper, and nutmeg; mix until well blended. Pour dressing over salad; add nuts and mix lightly until well coated. Serve immediately. Makes 6 servings.

Per serving: 287 calories, 6 grams protein, 9 grams carbohydrates, 28 grams total fat, 0 milligram cholesterol, 219 milligrams sodium.

Spinach & Enoki Salad

The crisp texture and mild, slightly tangy taste of enoki mushrooms are best appreciated raw—as in this spinach salad. Originally from Japan, these tiny, long-stemmed mushrooms are now widely cultivated.

1½ **pounds spinach, washed and crisped**
1 **or 2 packages (3½ oz. *each*) enoki mushrooms**
1 **cup cherry tomatoes, halved**
1 **carrot, thinly sliced**
2 **green onions, thinly sliced**
¼ **cup sugar**
⅓ **cup white wine vinegar**
¼ **teaspoon salt**
2 **tablespoons salad oil**

Remove and discard coarse spinach stems. Tear leaves into bite-size pieces (you should have about 3 quarts). Trim limp stem ends from enoki; rinse mushrooms and drain well. In a salad bowl, combine spinach, enoki, tomatoes, carrot, and onions. In a small bowl, combine sugar, vinegar, salt, and oil; mix until sugar dissolves. Pour dressing over salad and mix lightly until well coated. Serve immediately. Makes 6 to 8 servings.

Per serving: 82 calories, 3 grams protein, 12 grams carbohydrates, 4 grams total fat, 0 milligram cholesterol, 123 milligrams sodium.

FIRST-COURSE SALADS

Served as a first course, a flavorful salad gets a dinner party off to an appetizing start. Here, colorful accents lend pizzazz to green salads.

Chef's-style Endive Salad

Though the ingredients are familiar—greens, meat, cheese, and eggs—the presentation of this chef's salad will come as a surprise.

> **Watercress Dressing**
> **(recipe follows)**
> 3 **heads Belgian endive, washed and crisped**
> 2 **ounces Swiss cheese**
> 6 **paper-thin slices pastrami**
> 3 **hard-cooked eggs, cut in half lengthwise**
> **Watercress sprigs**

Prepare Watercress Dressing; spoon dressing into individual salad plates, making a shallow pool.

Cut heads of endive in half lengthwise, removing any discoloration from root ends. Separate each half into 3 sections and arrange side-by-side on plates.

Cut cheese into 18 thin strips and place a strip in each section of endive. Drape a slice of pastrami over each serving. Garnish with egg and watercress. Makes 6 servings.

Watercress Dressing. In a medium-size bowl, combine ¾ cup **sour cream;** ¼ cup **milk;** 2 tablespoons *each* **cider vinegar** and chopped **watercress leaves;** ½ teaspoon *each* **Dijon mustard, sugar,** and **dry tarragon;** and 1 clove **garlic,** minced or pressed. Mix until well blended.

Per serving: 164 calories, 10 grams protein, 5 grams carbohydrates, 12 grams total fat, 165 milligrams cholesterol, 274 milligrams sodium.

Vintner's Salad

Poached in wine, eggs take on a pink tinge. They're served warm atop greens that are tossed in a hot bacon dressing.

> **French Bread Croutons**
> **(recipe follows)**
> 6 **thick slices bacon, cut into 1-inch squares**
> 4 **eggs**
> 3 **cups dry red wine**
> 1 **quart *each* loosely packed torn inner leaves curly endive and green leaf lettuce, washed and crisped**
> 3 **tablespoons red wine vinegar**
> ¼ **teaspoon *each* sugar and white pepper**
> 1 **teaspoon Dijon mustard**

Prepare French Bread Croutons; keep warm.

In a wide frying pan, cook bacon over medium heat until crisp and browned (8 to 10 minutes). Lift out and drain, reserving ⅓ cup of the drippings in pan. Set drippings aside; keep bacon warm.

In a small pan, bring enough water to cover an egg to a boil over high heat. Place eggs, 1 at a time, in water for 8 seconds *each* to heat-set.

Heat wine in a deep greased frying pan over high heat until wine begins to bubble gently. Reduce heat to maintain this temperature. Break heat-set eggs into wine; poach, uncovered, until whites are firm (3 to 5 minutes). With a slotted spoon, remove eggs and drain briefly. Keep warm.

Place salad greens in a large bowl; set aside.

Add vinegar, sugar, pepper, and mustard to reserved drippings in pan. Place over medium heat and stir until heated through and well blended. Immediately pour hot dressing over greens; mix lightly until well coated.

Quickly arrange greens on individual plates; top each serving with a poached egg and sprinkle with bacon. Garnish with croutons and serve immediately. Makes 4 servings.

French Bread Croutons. Cut 16 thin slices from a **French bread baguette.** Arrange in a single layer on a baking sheet. Combine 1 tablespoon **butter** or margarine and 1 tablespoon **olive oil** in a small pan over medium heat; add 1 small clove **garlic,** sliced. Heat until butter is melted. Brush bread with butter mixture. Bake in a 250° oven until crisp and golden brown (40 to 45 minutes). If made ahead, reheat croutons in a 250° oven.

Per serving: 457 calories, 15 grams protein, 22 grams carbohydrates, 34 grams total fat, 308 milligrams cholesterol, 659 milligrams sodium.

Hazelnut & Chard Salad

Almost always served as a cooked green vegetable, red or green Swiss chard can also be enjoyed in a dinner salad. Another delicious innovation is the hazelnut dressing.

- ¼ **cup hazelnuts (filberts)**
- ¾ **pound Swiss chard, washed and crisped**
- 1 **package (3½ oz.) enoki mushrooms or 1 cup slivered regular mushrooms**
- ⅓ **cup olive oil or salad oil**
- 2 **tablespoons sherry vinegar or red wine vinegar**
  Salt and pepper
- 2 **teaspoons *each* minced red, green, and yellow bell pepper, or 2 tablespoons of any one bell pepper**

Place nuts in a shallow baking pan and toast in a 350° oven until pale golden beneath skins (8 to 10 minutes). Rub nuts together in a towel to remove as much as possible of skins. Let cool; then coarsely chop and set aside.

Remove and discard coarse chard stems. Chop leaves into ½-inch pieces. Trim limp stem ends from enoki; rinse mushrooms and drain well.

In a large bowl, mix oil, vinegar, and chopped nuts. Add chard and mix lightly until well coated; season with salt and pepper to taste.

Mound chard mixture onto individual salad plates. Arrange a cluster of mushrooms beside chard. Sprinkle mushrooms with minced bell pepper. Serve immediately. Makes 4 servings.

Per serving: 234 calories, 3 grams protein, 6 grams carbohydrates, 23 grams total fat, 0 milligram cholesterol, 202 milligrams sodium.

Coleslaw with Kuminost

Savory with caraway and cumin seeds, kuminost cheese adds flavor and substance to this crisp, multi-vegetable salad, an appetizing choice for a light meal.

- ¼ **cup *each* sour cream and mayonnaise**
- 1 **teaspoon Dijon mustard**
- 1½ **tablespoons white wine vinegar**
- ¼ **teaspoon *each* ground cumin and salt**
- ⅛ **teaspoon pepper**
- 2½ **cups thinly shredded cabbage**
- 1 **medium-size carrot, shredded**
- ½ **green bell pepper, seeded and cut into thin strips**

- 1 **cup thinly sliced green onions**
- ½ **cup diced dill pickles**
- 4 **to 5 ounces kuminost cheese, diced**

Combine sour cream, mayonnaise, mustard, vinegar, cumin, salt, and pepper; mix until well blended.

In a salad bowl, combine cabbage, carrot, bell pepper, onions, pickles, and cheese. Pour dressing over salad and mix lightly until well coated. Makes 2 or 3 main-dish or 4 to 6 first-course servings.

Per main-dish serving: 391 calories, 14 grams protein, 11 grams carbohydrates, 33 grams total fat, 61 milligrams cholesterol, 988 milligrams sodium.

Confetti Coleslaw

A tart-sweet dressing of yogurt and mayonnaise gives this colorful coleslaw fewer calories than the usual deli fare. Using a food processor to prepare this salad will save a lot of time.

- 1 **small head red or green cabbage (about 1¼ lbs.), shredded**
- 2 **large carrots, shredded**
- 2 **medium-size tart apples, chopped**
- 4 **green onions, thinly sliced**
- 1 **cup plain yogurt**
- ¼ **cup mayonnaise**
- 3 **tablespoons white wine vinegar**
- 1 **tablespoon sugar**
- ½ **teaspoon dry tarragon**
  Salt and pepper

In a salad bowl, combine cabbage, carrots, apples, and onions. (At this point, you may cover and refrigerate for up to 2 hours.) In a medium-size bowl, combine yogurt, mayonnaise, vinegar, sugar, and tarragon; mix until well blended.

Just before serving, pour dressing over cabbage mixture and mix lightly until well coated. Season with salt and pepper to taste. Serve immediately. Makes 6 servings.

Per serving: 158 calories, 4 grams protein, 20 grams carbohydrates, 8 grams total fat, 8 milligrams cholesterol, 119 milligrams sodium.

Confetti Coleslaw

Bright chunks of apple are tossed amid ribbonlike strands of cabbage for a festive salad.

Zucchini-Apple Slaw

What to do with nature's summertime bounty? Indulge in a refreshing and unusual salad of zucchini and apples.

Place pan with drippings over high heat and stir in orange juice, vinegar, and sugar. Cook just until drippings are melted and dressing is hot. Immediately pour hot dressing over salad and mix quickly until well coated.

Place a whole cabbage leaf on each of 6 salad plates; mound salad on each leaf. Garnish with reserved mint. Makes 6 servings.

Per serving: 154 calories, 5 grams protein, 8 grams carbohydrates, 12 grams total fat, 9 milligrams cholesterol, 163 milligrams sodium.

Napa-Mint Slaw

Crinkly napa cabbage (also known as Chinese cabbage) and cool fresh mint combine with a warm bacon and orange dressing to make this welcome winter salad.

> 5 **slices bacon, chopped**
> **Salad oil (optional)**
> 1 **medium-size head napa cabbage (about 1½ lbs.), washed and crisped**
> 1 **cup lightly packed fresh mint leaves or ¼ cup dry mint**
> ⅓ **cup chopped roasted, salted peanuts**
> ⅓ **cup orange juice**
> 3 **tablespoons white wine vinegar**
> 1½ **teaspoons sugar**

In an 8- to 10-inch frying pan, cook bacon over medium heat until crisp (about 8 minutes). Lift out and drain; set aside. Discard all but 3 tablespoons of the drippings from pan (add oil, if necessary, to make 3 tablespoons); set pan aside.

Remove 6 large outer leaves from cabbage and set aside. Cut head of cabbage crosswise into ¼-inch slices. Setting aside 6 fresh mint sprigs for garnish, finely chop remaining mint. Combine with cabbage, peanuts, and bacon in a large bowl.

Zucchini-Apple Slaw

There's no cabbage in this slaw—just crisp zucchini and apples—but it's sure to become a summertime favorite.

> ½ **cup mayonnaise**
> 3 **tablespoons cider vinegar**
> 1 **tablespoon sugar**
> 1 **teaspoon caraway seeds**
> 4 **cups coarsely shredded zucchini**
> ¼ **cup thinly sliced green onions**
> 2 **to 3 medium-size red- or green-skinned tart apples**
> **Salt and pepper**

Combine mayonnaise, vinegar, sugar, and caraway seeds; mix until well blended.

In a large bowl, combine zucchini and onions. Core apples, peel if desired, and cut into ½-inch chunks (you should have about 3 cups). Add apples to zucchini mixture; pour dressing over salad and mix lightly until well coated. Season with salt and pepper to taste. Cover and refrigerate for at least 2 hours or up to 4 hours. With a slotted spoon, transfer salad to a serving bowl. Makes 6 servings.

Per serving: 186 calories, 1 gram protein, 14 grams carbohydrates, 15 grams total fat, 11 milligrams cholesterol, 107 milligrams sodium.

Caesar-style Vegetable Salad

A spirited Caesar dressing transforms a generous assortment of crisp raw vegetables into an exciting salad.

Autumn Slaw

Don't restrict yourself to autumn to serve this salad —it's a sumptuous choice for a buffet or potluck at any time of year.

- 1 **medium-size head green cabbage (about 2 lbs.), finely shredded**
- 1 **teaspoon salt**
- 1¼ **cups** *each* **sugar and water**
- 1 **cup vinegar**
- 3 **cups thinly sliced celery**
- 1 **large red or green bell pepper, seeded and chopped**
- ½ **cup thinly sliced green onions**
- 1 **teaspoon** *each* **celery seeds and mustard seeds**

Place cabbage in a large bowl, sprinkle with salt, and let stand for 2 hours.

Meanwhile, combine sugar, water, and vinegar in a 1½- to 2-quart pan. Bring to a boil over high heat, stirring until sugar dissolves; boil for 2 minutes. Remove from heat; let cool to room temperature.

Drain and discard any liquid from cabbage. In a large bowl, combine cabbage, celery, bell pepper, onions, celery seeds, mustard seeds, and vinegar mixture; mix until moistened. Cover and refrigerate for at least 24 hours or up to a week.

With a slotted spoon, transfer salad to a serving bowl. Makes 10 to 12 servings (about 2½ quarts).

Per serving: 107 calories, 1 gram protein, 27 grams carbohydrates, .28 gram total fat, 0 milligram cholesterol, 222 milligrams sodium.

Caesar-style Vegetable Salad

A colorful assortment of raw vegetables comes to life with the addition of a Caesar-style dressing in this spectacular salad.

- 1 **small bunch broccoli (about 1 lb.)**
- 1 **small head cauliflower (about 1 lb.)**
- 1 **small zucchini**
- 2 **large carrots**
- ¼ **pound mushrooms, thinly sliced**
- 1 **small red or green bell pepper, seeded and cut into matchstick pieces**
  Caesar Dressing (recipe follows)
- 1 **egg**
- ¾ **cup grated Parmesan cheese**

Cut broccoli flowerets into bite-size pieces and stalks into paper-thin slices. Cut cauliflower flowerets into bite-size pieces. Cut zucchini and carrots into paper-thin slices.

In a salad bowl, combine broccoli, cauliflower, zucchini, carrots, mushrooms, and bell pepper.

Prepare Caesar Dressing. Just before serving, beat egg and add to vegetables. Pour dressing over salad and sprinkle with cheese; mix lightly until well coated. Serve immediately. Makes 6 to 8 servings.

Caesar Dressing. Mix until blended ¾ cup **olive oil** or salad oil; 6 tablespoons **lemon juice;** 2 cloves **garlic,** minced or pressed; 6 to 8 canned **anchovy fillets,** drained well and chopped; ¾ teaspoon **pepper;** and 1½ teaspoons **Worcestershire.**

Per serving: 266 calories, 7 grams protein, 8 grams carbohydrates, 24 grams total fat, 42 milligrams cholesterol, 216 milligrams sodium.

Broccoli & Cheddar Cheese Salad

In this show-stopping salad, broccoli flowerets are boldly accented by strips of cheese and slices of mushroom. Chives and pine nuts add colorful highlights.

- ¾ **pound broccoli**
- 2 **tablespoons pine nuts**
- 4 **ounces Cheddar cheese, cut into matchstick pieces**
- ¼ **pound medium-size mushrooms, thinly sliced**
  Chive Dressing (recipe follows)

Cut off broccoli stem ends and, if desired, peel stalks. Cut flowerets from stalks and cut stalks crosswise into thin slices. Arrange broccoli on a steamer rack; steam, covered, over 1 inch of boiling water until barely tender when pierced (about 5 minutes). Rinse broccoli with cold water and drain well.

Meanwhile, toast nuts in a small frying pan over medium heat, shaking pan often, until nuts are golden (3 to 5 minutes).

In a salad bowl, combine broccoli, cheese, and mushrooms. Prepare Chive Dressing; pour over salad and mix lightly until well coated. Sprinkle with nuts. Serve immediately. Makes 4 servings.

Chive Dressing. Combine ¼ cup **olive oil** or salad oil, 3 tablespoons **lemon juice,** 2 tablespoons minced **chives** or green onions, ¼ teaspoon *each* **garlic salt** and **dry mustard,** and ⅛ teaspoon **white pepper;** mix until well blended.

Per serving: 282 calories, 10 grams protein, 6 grams carbohydrates, 26 grams total fat, 30 milligrams cholesterol, 307 milligrams sodium.

Zucchini Noodles with Two Dressings

Zucchini strands masquerade as green pasta in this innovative salad. Served with contrasting dressings, it offers a dramatic first course.

- **Raspberry Dressing (recipe follows)**
- **Green or Gold Pepper Dressing (recipe follows)**
- 1 **pound medium-size zucchini**
- 1 *each* **lemon and lime,** *each* **cut into 6 wedges**
  Watercress sprigs

Prepare Raspberry Dressing and Green or Gold Pepper Dressing; set aside.

With a knife, coarse shredder, or Oriental shredder fitted with a fine or coarse blade, cut zucchini lengthwise into long, very thin slivers. Dividing zucchini equally, mound in center of individual salad plates. (At this point, you may cover and refrigerate for up to 5 hours.)

On each plate, spoon about 2 tablespoons of the Raspberry Dressing halfway around zucchini; spoon an equal amount of the Pepper Dressing on opposite side of plate. Garnish each serving with a lemon and lime wedge and with watercress. Makes 6 servings.

Raspberry Dressing. In a 1-quart pan, melt 1 tablespoon **raspberry jam** or jelly over high heat, stirring constantly; remove from heat and stir in 3 tablespoons **red wine vinegar.** Add ½ cup **salad oil** and 1 tablespoon minced **shallot** or red onion; mix well. Season with **salt** and **pepper** to taste. If made ahead, cover and refrigerate for up to 2 days.

Green or Gold Pepper Dressing. In a food processor or blender, combine ⅓ cup **olive oil** or salad oil, ⅓ cup seeded, diced **green or yellow bell pepper,** and 1 tablespoon minced **shallot.** Whirl until pepper is puréed. Season to taste with **ground red pepper** (cayenne). If made ahead, cover and refrigerate until next day.

Just before serving, blend in 2 tablespoons **white wine vinegar** and season with **salt** and **pepper** to taste.

Per serving: 298 calories, 1 gram protein, 9 grams carbohydrates, 30 grams total fat, 0 milligram cholesterol, 50 milligrams sodium.

Broccoli & Cheddar Cheese Salad

A visual feast, this colorful salad is bathed in a tart dressing flavored with lemon and chives.

Green Bean & Zucchini Bundles

For an enticing presentation at a summer buffet, serve tender-crisp beans inside rings of zucchini. Dress each portion with a basil-honey vinaigrette.

1½ **pounds thin green beans**
1 **medium-size zucchini, at least 2 inches in diameter**
½ **cup salad oil**
¼ **cup white wine vinegar**
2 **tablespoons** *each* **Dijon mustard and honey**
2 **small cloves garlic, minced or pressed**
2 **tablespoons chopped fresh basil leaves or 2 teaspoons dry basil**

Remove ends and strings from beans; set aside. Cut zucchini crosswise into 8 equal slices. With a small knife, carve out centers of zucchini slices, leaving a ¼-inch rim (reserve zucchini centers for other uses, if desired).

Arrange beans on a steamer rack; steam, covered, over 1 inch of boiling water just until tender-crisp when pierced (5 to 8 minutes). Immediately immerse in ice water to cool.

Add zucchini to steamer; steam, covered, over 1 inch of boiling water just until tender when pierced (2 to 3 minutes). Immerse in ice water. Drain vegetables well.

Insert 8 to 10 beans through each zucchini ring. Arrange bundles in a shallow dish. (At this point, you may cover and refrigerate until next day.)

Combine oil, vinegar, mustard, honey, garlic, and basil; mix until well blended. Spoon dressing equally over bean bundles. Makes 8 servings.

Per serving: 169 calories, 2 grams protein, 11 grams carbohydrates, 14 grams total fat, 0 milligram cholesterol, 118 milligrams sodium.

Roasted Bell Peppers (recipe follows) or 2 jars (7 oz. *each*) roasted red peppers
2 **large heads garlic**
16 **to 20 mushrooms (about 2 inches in diameter)**
3 **medium-size zucchini, cut into ½-inch-thick slanting slices**
1 **cup olive oil**
2 **tablespoons lemon juice**
Salt and pepper
12 **thin slices French bread baguette**
Niçoise or ripe olives
1 **can (2 oz.) anchovy fillets, drained well**

Prepare Roasted Bell Peppers; set aside.

Cut each head of garlic in half crosswise. Place garlic heads, cut sides down, in a shallow 10- by 15-inch baking pan; arrange mushrooms and zucchini in a single layer alongside. Pour oil and lemon juice over vegetables; sprinkle lightly with salt and pepper. Roast, uncovered, in a 350° oven until garlic is golden on bottom (about 40 minutes).

Just before serving, place bread slices in a single layer on a rack in a 350° oven. Bake until dry (about 10 minutes). Remove from oven and set aside.

With a slotted spoon, lift out roasted vegetables from oil. Arrange vegetables, bell peppers, bread, olives, and anchovies on individual dinner plates. Drizzle remaining oil mixture over all. To eat, pluck out softened garlic with a fork; spread on bread slices or combine with other vegetables. Makes 4 servings.

Roasted Bell Peppers. Set 4 large red, yellow, or green **bell peppers** in a 9-inch square baking pan. Broil 1 inch from heat, turning occasionally, until charred on all sides (about 30 minutes). Cover pan and let stand until peppers are cool. Pull off and discard skin. Cut peppers open; discard stem and seeds. If made ahead, cover and refrigerate for up to 3 days.

Per serving: 512 calories, 9 grams protein, 36 grams carbohydrates, 39 grams total fat, 5 milligrams cholesterol, 276 milligrams sodium.

Rustic Roasted Vegetable Salad

Robustly flavored roasted vegetables, accompanied by sharp cheese and red wine, make a satisfying supper. The vegetables bake in a lemon-accented oil that becomes a mellow dressing. The salad can be cooked as long as a day ahead, refrigerated, then served at room temperature.

Shredded Carrots with Turnip

When the price of lettuce soars in winter, look no further than to such familiar root vegetables as carrots and turnips to make a crisp, attractive salad.

2 **cups coarsely shredded carrots**
1½ **cups peeled, coarsely shredded turnips**
¼ **cup thinly sliced green onions**

½ cup chopped parsley
6 pitted ripe olives or green olives, sliced
¼ cup lemon juice
¼ cup olive oil or salad oil
½ teaspoon *each* salt and dry mustard

In a salad bowl, combine carrots, turnips, onions, parsley, and olives (reserve some olive slices for garnish, if desired). In a small bowl, mix lemon juice, oil, salt, and mustard. Pour dressing over salad and mix lightly until well coated. Cover and refrigerate until chilled (about 45 minutes).

Just before serving, mix salad again. Garnish, if desired, with reserved olive slices. Makes 4 to 6 servings.

Per serving: 116 calories, .95 gram protein, 7 grams carbohydrates, 10 grams total fat, 0 milligram cholesterol, 248 milligrams sodium.

Pea & Peanut Salad

An adventure of contrasting flavors and textures, this salad nestles in crisp lettuce leaves. Offer it as an appetizer or as a more formal first course.

8 slices bacon
1 package (10 oz.) frozen tiny peas, thawed
4 stalks celery, finely chopped
1 small onion, finely chopped
1½ cups roasted, salted peanuts
½ cup mayonnaise
½ cup plain yogurt or sour cream
2 tablespoons lemon juice
⅛ to ¼ teaspoon ground red pepper (cayenne)
About 24 small butter or romaine lettuce leaves, washed and crisped

In a wide frying pan, cook bacon over medium heat until crisp. Lift out, drain, and crumble coarsely; set aside.

In a large bowl, combine peas, celery, onion, peanuts, mayonnaise, yogurt, and lemon juice; mix until combined. Season with red pepper to taste.

Transfer salad to a serving bowl and sprinkle with bacon. Serve lettuce alongside, spooning salad into lettuce leaves to eat out of hand. Or arrange lettuce on individual plates and spoon salad into leaves to eat with a fork. Makes 6 to 8 appetizer servings, 3 or 4 first-course servings.

Per serving: 334 calories, 12 grams protein, 12 grams carbohydrates, 28 grams total fat, 14 milligrams cholesterol, 374 milligrams sodium.

Flowering Salads

The bright blossoms of herbs and edible flowers make dramatic garnishes for summer salads.

The flowers and leaves of nasturtiums have a peppery flavor somewhat akin to that of watercress; yet an area at the base of each blossom is quite sweet. For a colorful accent to a potato salad with a creamy vinaigrette dressing, chop nasturtium leaves and a few blossoms, and sprinkle them over the salad. Or try whole petals in an arranged salad with red leaf lettuce, seedless grapes, and an oil and vinegar dressing.

When fresh herbs bloom, use their flowers as a salad ingredient to complement the herb in the dressing. The purplish flowers of basil and chives are especially attractive.

The yellow flowers of arugula (rocket) are also edible; they have a mustardy tang resembling that of the leaf.

The petals of roses, carnations, marigolds, and violets, flowers usually grown for their color and fragrance, lend flavor and character to green and fruit salads.

Be absolutely sure that the flowers you use are edible and that they're well rinsed to remove any clinging dust or pesticides. Wash, pat dry, and refrigerate the flowers as you would delicate herbs and salad greens; they'll keep in the refrigerator for up to a day. ■

Fresh Asparagus Victor

Whole asparagus spears substitute for celery in this springtime version of the famous marinated salad created by Chef Victor Hirtzler of the St. Francis Hotel in San Francisco.

1 can (14½ oz.) regular-strength chicken broth

2 pounds asparagus, tough ends removed

6 tablespoons olive oil or salad oil

¼ cup white wine vinegar

2 tablespoons *each* finely chopped green onion and pimentos

1 teaspoon Dijon mustard

¼ teaspoon salt

⅛ teaspoon pepper
  Shredded iceberg lettuce

2 hard-cooked eggs, quartered

8 to 12 cherry tomatoes, halved
  Pitted ripe olives

1 can (2 oz.) anchovy fillets, well drained (optional)

In a large frying pan, bring chicken broth to a boil over high heat. Add asparagus; reduce heat, cover, and simmer until tender when pierced (7 to 9 minutes). Using tongs, lift out asparagus and arrange in a single layer in a wide, shallow bowl. (Reserve broth for other uses, if desired.)

In a small bowl, combine oil, vinegar, onion, pimento, mustard, salt, and pepper; mix until well blended. Pour dressing over asparagus. Cover and refrigerate for at least 4 hours or up to 6 hours.

Arrange lettuce on a large platter. Layer asparagus on top and garnish with eggs, tomatoes, olives, and, if desired, anchovies. Drizzle with remaining dressing. Makes 4 to 6 servings.

Per serving: 179 calories, 5 grams protein, 5 grams carbohydrates, 16 grams total fat, 91 milligrams cholesterol, 447 milligrams sodium.

Leeks in Creamy Tarragon Dressing

Colorful strips of chives and red and yellow peppers scatter like confetti across these tender, poached leeks—as lovely to view as to taste.

9 to 12 small to medium-size leeks

3 tablespoons white wine vinegar

1 tablespoon lemon juice

1 teaspoon Dijon mustard

1 egg yolk

¼ cup fresh tarragon leaves or 1 tablespoon dry tarragon and ¼ cup chopped parsley

1 clove garlic, minced or pressed

¼ teaspoon salt

⅛ teaspoon pepper

¼ cup olive oil

½ cup salad oil

⅓ cup thin, 1½-inch-long red and yellow bell pepper strips

2 tablespoons 1½-inch-long chive strips

Cut off and discard root ends of leeks. Trim tops, leaving about 2 inches of dark green leaves. Discard coarse outer leaves. Cut leeks in half lengthwise. Hold each half under cold running water, separating layers to rinse out dirt.

Place leeks in a single layer in a wide frying pan; add water to cover. Bring water to a boil over high heat; reduce heat, cover, and simmer just until stem ends are tender when pierced (3 to 5 minutes). Lift out leeks, being careful to keep each half intact; let cool to room temperature. (At this point, you may cover and refrigerate until next day.)

Meanwhile, in a blender or food processor, combine vinegar, lemon juice, mustard, egg yolk, tarragon, garlic, salt, and pepper. Whirl until tarragon is puréed; turn off motor. Add olive oil and salad oil all at once. Whirl until oil is incorporated and dressing is well blended. If made ahead, cover and refrigerate until next day.

Pour dressing into individual salad plates or a rimmed platter. Arrange leek halves on plates and sprinkle with bell peppers and chives. Serve immediately. Makes 6 servings.

Per serving: 320 calories, 2 grams protein, 16 grams carbohydrates, 29 grams total fat, 45 milligrams cholesterol, 140 milligrams sodium.

Leeks in Creamy Tarragon Dressing

Chives and peppers add bright, festive accents to tender poached leeks in this exquisitely designed salad.

Whole Cauliflower Salad

For a light, lovely, and dramatic winter salad, serve a whole head of tender, marinated cauliflower.

Combine basil, oregano, and fennel seeds in a large tea ball, or tie in a triple thickness of cheesecloth. Place in a 2- to 3-quart pan along with broth; bring to a boil over high heat. Add lentils; reduce heat, cover, and simmer until lentils are tender to bite (25 to 30 minutes). Drain lentils, discarding herbs. (Reserve broth for other uses, if desired.)

Rinse kidney beans and drain well. In a serving bowl, combine beans and cooked lentils. Prepare Red Pepper Dressing; pour over bean mixture and mix lightly until well coated. Season with salt and pepper to taste. Cover and refrigerate for at least 6 hours or until next day.

Stir parsley into lentil mixture. Surround salad with lettuce and endive leaves. Makes 6 servings.

Red Pepper Dressing. Combine ⅔ cup **olive oil** or salad oil, ½ cup *each* finely chopped **red bell pepper** and **onion**, ¼ cup **white wine vinegar**, and 1½ tablespoons **Dijon mustard.** Mix until well blended.

Per serving: 423 calories, 14 grams protein, 34 grams carbohydrates, 26 grams total fat, 0 milligram cholesterol, 933 milligrams sodium.

White Bean & Lentil Salad

Serve this substantial salad in a bowl or basket generously lined with crisp greens. Accompany it with sausage or pâté, crusty bread, and your favorite cheeses.

- **2 teaspoons *each* dry basil, oregano leaves, and fennel seeds**
- **2 cups regular-strength chicken broth**
- **½ cup dried lentils, sorted, rinsed, and drained**
- **2 cans (15 oz. *each*) white kidney beans (cannellini), drained**
- **Red Pepper Dressing (recipe follows)**
- **Salt and pepper**
- **¼ cup finely chopped parsley**
- **1 small head *each* romaine and red leaf lettuce, washed and crisped**
- **1 medium-size head Belgian endive (optional), washed and crisped**

Whole Cauliflower Salad

Steamed, then marinated in a lemony dressing, a whole cauliflower makes a handsome winter salad to serve cold or at room temperature.

- **1 medium-size head cauliflower (about 1½ lbs.)**
- **¼ cup lemon juice**
- **¼ cup olive oil or salad oil**
- **½ teaspoon *each* thyme leaves and dry mustard**

Garbanzo & Walnut Salad

Crisp leaves of romaine lettuce make
perfect scoopers for this lemony
garbanzo salad.

1 teaspoon salt
⅛ teaspoon white pepper
Radish roses or sliced radishes
Parsley sprigs or chopped parsley

Cut off cauliflower stem. Place whole cauliflower on
a steamer rack; steam, covered, over 1 inch boiling
water until tender when pierced (about 10 minutes).
Rinse with cold water and drain well.

In a deep bowl, combine lemon juice, oil, thyme,
mustard, salt, and pepper; mix until well blended.
Add cauliflower, turning several times until well
coated with dressing. Cover and marinate for at least
2 hours at room temperature or, if refrigerated, until
next day, turning cauliflower several times.

Place cauliflower on a rimmed platter and
drizzle with some of the dressing. Garnish with
radishes and parsley. Offer remaining dressing
at the table to add to individual servings. Makes
6 servings.

*Per serving: 11 calories, .88 gram protein, 2 grams
carbohydrates, .08 gram total fat, 0 milligram cholesterol,
7 milligrams sodium.*

*Per tablespoon of dressing: 62 calories, .05 gram protein, .57
gram carbohydrates, 7 grams total fat, 0 milligram cholesterol,
277 milligrams sodium.*

Garbanzo & Walnut Salad

For a quick and easy salad or an informal appetizer,
serve this blend of garbanzos and walnuts in a
lemon-garlic dressing.

Lemon Dressing (recipe follows)
1 can (about 1 lb.) garbanzos, drained
⅔ cup finely chopped walnuts
**Small inner leaves of 2 heads romaine
lettuce, washed and crisped**

Prepare Lemon Dressing. In a bowl, mash garbanzos
until coarsely crumbled; stir in walnuts. Add dressing
and mix until well blended. If made ahead, cover
and refrigerate for up to 6 hours; let come to room
temperature before serving.

Spoon salad into center of a shallow bowl or
rimmed platter; surround with lettuce leaves to use
as scoopers. Makes about 6 appetizer servings.

Lemon Dressing. In a small bowl, combine 6 tablespoons **lemon juice;** ¼ cup **olive oil** or salad oil;
2 cloves **garlic,** minced or pressed; and 1 teaspoon
salt. Mix until well blended.

*Per serving: 249 calories, 7 grams protein, 16 grams
carbohydrates, 19 grams total fat, 0 milligram cholesterol,
608 milligrams sodium.*

Rouge et Noir Salad

As a salad green, peppery watercress sprigs offer a piquant foil for tomatoes, mushrooms, and olives in this colorful red-and-black salad.

> 2 **bunches watercress (¾ to 1 lb. *total*), washed and crisped**
> ¾ **pound mushrooms, sliced**
> 1 **can (3½ oz.) pitted ripe olives, drained**
> 18 **cherry tomatoes, halved**
> 1 **egg yolk**
> ¼ **cup lemon juice**
> ½ **teaspoon *each* sugar and dry basil**
> ¼ **teaspoon *each* salt and ground nutmeg**
> ⅛ **teaspoon white pepper**
> ½ **cup salad oil**

Remove and discard coarse watercress stems (you should have about 1½ quarts). In a large bowl, combine watercress, mushrooms, olives, and tomatoes. Cover and refrigerate for at least 2 hours or up to 4 hours.

In a blender or food processor, combine egg yolk, lemon juice, sugar, basil, salt, nutmeg, and pepper; whirl until smooth. With motor running, slowly pour in oil and whirl until thickened. If made ahead, cover and refrigerate for at least 2 hours or up to 4 hours.

Arrange salad on individual plates and drizzle with dressing. Serve immediately. Makes 6 servings.

Per serving: 127 calories, 4 grams protein, 6 grams carbohydrates, 11 grams total fat, 21 milligrams cholesterol, 150 milligrams sodium.

Tomatoes & Gorgonzola with Black Beans

If you have leftover fermented black beans from a Chinese cooking spree, you'll enjoy their pungent, slightly sweet flavor in this sprightly salad.

Rouge et Noir Salad

Bright red cherry tomato halves and shiny black olives sparkle from a bed of tender watercress.

> 3 **large firm-ripe tomatoes, cored and sliced**
> 1 **tablespoon minced shallots or mild onion**
> ⅛ **teaspoon freshly ground pepper**
> ½ **cup (2 oz.) crumbled Gorgonzola**
> 2 **tablespoons fermented black beans**
>   **Watercress sprigs**
>   **Olive oil or salad oil**
>   **Red wine vinegar**

Overlap sliced tomatoes at one end of a serving platter. Sprinkle with shallots and pepper; mound cheese alongside. In a wire strainer, rinse black beans; drain well. Arrange beans next to cheese; garnish platter with watercress. Pass cruets of oil and vinegar at the table. Makes 6 servings.

Per serving: 70 calories, 4 grams protein, 6 grams carbohydrates, 4 grams total fat, 8 milligrams cholesterol, 395 milligrams sodium.

Tri-mustard Tomato Salad

Three forms of mustard boldly season this crisp mixed salad. It's a refreshing choice for a summer picnic.

> 1 **medium-size cucumber**
> 1 **medium-size green bell pepper**
> 1 **medium-size red onion**
> 4 **large firm-ripe tomatoes**
>   **Tri-mustard Vinaigrette (recipe follows)**
>   **Salt and pepper**

Score cucumber skin lengthwise with a fork, or peel. Cut into ¼-inch-thick slices. Cut bell pepper in half lengthwise and discard stem and seeds; then cut crosswise into ¼-inch-thick slices. Thinly slice onion and separate into rings. Core tomatoes and cut into ½-inch-thick wedges.

Prepare Tri-mustard Vinaigrette. In a salad bowl, combine cucumber, bell pepper, onion, tomatoes, and dressing; mix lightly until well coated. Season with salt and pepper to taste. Makes 6 to 8 servings.

Tri-mustard Vinaigrette. Mix ¼ cup **salad oil,** 2 tablespoons **white wine vinegar,** 2 tablespoons *each* **Dijon mustard** and **mustard seeds,** 2 teaspoons **dry mustard,** and ½ to 1 teaspoon **liquid hot pepper seasoning.**

Per serving: 104 calories, 2 grams protein, 7 grams carbohydrates, 8 grams total fat, 0 milligram cholesterol, 152 milligrams sodium.

Mediterranean Tomato Salad

For a light summertime meal, accompany these tomatoes with canned stuffed grape leaves, a mild cheese—such as jack or string cheese—and nectarines or plums.

        ¼ cup salad oil
    1½ tablespoons lemon juice
        2 teaspoons white wine vinegar
        1 small clove garlic, minced or pressed
            (optional)
        ½ teaspoon *each* salt and pepper
        1 can (15 oz.) garbanzos, drained
        1 cup chopped red onion
        ¼ cup *each* chopped parsley and fresh mint
        4 large firm-ripe tomatoes

Combine oil, lemon juice, vinegar, garlic (if desired), salt, and pepper; mix until well blended. Add garbanzos, onion, parsley, and mint; mix lightly until well coated.

Cut tops off tomatoes; set tops aside. Scoop out seeds and pulp (reserve for other uses, if desired). Fill tomatoes with garbanzo mixture. Replace tops to serve. Makes 4 servings.

Per serving: 267 calories, 7 grams protein, 27 grams carbohydrates, 16 grams total fat, 0 milligram cholesterol, 635 milligrams sodium.

Sliced Tomatoes with Marinated Blanched Garlic

Blanching tames the strong flavor of garlic and reveals an underlying sweetness. To taste for yourself, serve generous portions of blanched garlic in a vinaigrette dressing over sliced tomatoes and lettuce.

        Blanched Garlic (recipe follows)
        ½ cup olive oil or salad oil
        3 tablespoons white wine vinegar
        1 tablespoon *each* finely chopped parsley
            and Dijon mustard
        Butter lettuce leaves, washed and crisped
        4 medium-size firm-ripe tomatoes,
            cored and sliced
        Salt and freshly ground pepper

Prepare Blanched Garlic. In a 1½- to 2-cup jar, combine oil, vinegar, parsley, and mustard, Add garlic; cover and shake until well blended. Let marinate at room temperature for at least 15 minutes or until next day.

Line a serving platter with lettuce leaves; arrange sliced tomatoes on top. Spoon garlic mixture over tomatoes; season with salt and pepper to taste. Serve immediately. Makes 6 to 8 servings.

Blanched Garlic. Break 2 heads **garlic** (about 3 inches in diameter *each*) apart into cloves. Drop cloves, unpeeled, into rapidly boiling water to cover. Boil, uncovered, until tender when pierced (3 minutes for ¼-inch-thick cloves to 10 minutes for 1-inch-thick cloves); drain well. When cool enough to handle, pinch tips of cloves between thumb and forefinger, squeezing garlic out of its skin. If made ahead, cover and refrigerate for up to a week. Makes about 1 cup.

Per serving: 150 calories, 1 gram protein, 6 grams carbohydrates, 14 grams total fat, 0 milligram cholesterol, 80 milligrams sodium.

Cannery Row Potato Salad

A restaurant on Monterey's Cannery Row long ago created this classic potato salad. Ripe olives, green onions, and pimentos give it festive character.

    3½ pounds medium-size red thin-skinned
            potatoes
        ½ cup olive oil or salad oil
        3 cloves garlic, chopped
        ¼ cup sweet pickle relish
        ½ cup mayonnaise
        1 can (2¼ oz.) sliced ripe olives, drained
        ½ cup *each* thinly sliced celery and
            green onions
        Salt and pepper
        1 jar (2 oz.) sliced pimentos, drained
        Chopped parsley

Scrub potatoes (do not peel). Place in a large pan with about 1 inch water. Cover and boil gently until potatoes are just tender when pierced (about 30 minutes); drain well. When cool enough to handle, cut into ½-inch cubes. Place in a large bowl.

Combine oil and garlic in a blender or food processor; whirl until garlic is puréed. Add to potatoes; mix lightly until well coated. Let stand until cool. Add pickle relish, mayonnaise, olives, celery, and onions; season with salt and pepper to taste. Mix lightly until thoroughly combined. Cover and refrigerate for at least 3 hours or until next day.

Just before serving, garnish salad with pimentos and parsley. Makes 8 to 10 servings.

Per serving: 325 calories, 4 grams protein, 32 grams carbohydrates, 21 grams total fat, 6 milligrams cholesterol, 184 milligrams sodium.

Midwinter Potato Salad

Standard fare for warm-season picnics, potato salad is just as welcome in winter. Red-skinned apples add color and juicy crispness to this salad dressed with savory blue cheese.

  2½ **pounds thin-skinned potatoes**
   ¾ **cup *each* mayonnaise and sour cream**
   4 **ounces (about 1 cup) blue-veined cheese, crumbled**
   1 **teaspoon salt**
   ½ **teaspoon dry basil**
   ¼ **teaspoon pepper**
   2 **large red-skinned apples**
   ¼ **cup lemon juice**
   1 **cup thinly sliced celery**
   ½ **cup coarsely chopped walnuts**

Scrub potatoes (do not peel). Place in a 3-quart pan with about 1 inch water. Cover and boil gently until potatoes are just tender when pierced (about 30 minutes); drain well and set aside.

In a medium-size bowl, combine mayonnaise, sour cream, cheese, salt, basil, and pepper; stir until well blended.

Core and dice apples (do not peel). Place in a large salad bowl; sprinkle with lemon juice and mix to coat cut edges. Peel potatoes, if desired, and dice. Add to apples along with celery. Pour dressing over salad and mix lightly until well coated. Cover and refrigerate for at least 3 hours or until next day.

Just before serving, sprinkle salad with walnuts. Makes 6 to 8 servings.

Per serving: 434 calories, 8 grams protein, 36 grams carbohydrates, 30 grams total fat, 32 milligrams cholesterol, 626 milligrams sodium.

Salad in a Pie

For an unconventional first course, this salad presents warm tomato sauce in a pastry shell, garnished with cool avocado slices and sour cream.

    Tart Shell (recipe follows)
   ½ **pound bacon, chopped**
   1 **medium-size onion, chopped**
   3 **firm-ripe tomatoes, chopped**
   1 **large can (7 oz.) diced green chiles**
   ½ **teaspoon ground cumin**
   1 **cup (4 oz.) shredded sharp Cheddar cheese**
   1 **medium-size ripe avocado**
   ⅓ **cup sour cream**
    Fresh cilantro (coriander) sprigs

Prepare Tart Shell; set aside.

In a wide frying pan, cook bacon over medium heat, stirring until crisp. Lift out, drain, and set aside, reserving 1 tablespoon of the drippings in pan. Add onion and cook, stirring until soft. Add tomatoes, green chiles, and cumin; cook, stirring until thick (about 15 minutes). Add bacon. Spoon into tart shell; sprinkle with cheese.

Bake in a 400° oven until cheese is melted (about 8 minutes). Pit, peel, and slice avocado. Arrange over tart; garnish with sour cream and cilantro. Makes 6 to 8 servings.

Tart Shell. In a food processor, combine 1½ cups **all-purpose flour** and ½ cup (¼ lb.) firm **butter** or margarine, cut into pieces. Process until mixture resembles fine crumbs. Add 1 **egg**; process until dough holds together.

Press pastry into a 9-inch tart pan or pie pan. Bake in a 325° oven until golden (about 45 minutes).

Per serving: 391 calories, 11 grams protein, 25 grams carbohydrates, 28 grams total fat, 92 milligrams cholesterol, 512 milligrams sodium.

Sacramento Bean Salad

This three-bean salad stands three steps above the usual version with the addition of marinated artichoke hearts, sliced carrots, and tangy dill pickles. It's a big salad that's perfect picnic fare—and you can make it in advance.

 2 cans (15 oz. *each*) kidney beans, drained
 1 can (6 oz.) pitted ripe olives, drained
 1 can (1 lb.) dilled green beans or
    cut green beans, drained
 1 jar (4 oz.) sliced pimentos, drained
 1 can (8 oz.) garbanzos, drained
 1 jar (6 oz.) marinated artichoke hearts
 1½ cups *each* thinly sliced celery and carrots
 2 large dill pickles, thinly sliced crosswise
 1 large mild red onion, thinly sliced
    Oil & Vinegar Dressing (recipe follows)
 2 hard-cooked eggs, sliced

In a large bowl, combine kidney beans, olives, green beans, pimentos, and garbanzos. Drain artichokes, reserving marinade. Cut artichokes in half lengthwise; set a few aside for garnish. Add remaining artichokes to bean mixture along with celery, carrots, pickles, and onion.

Prepare Oil & Vinegar Dressing. Pour over bean salad and mix lightly until well coated. Cover and refrigerate for at least 8 hours or until next day, stirring several times.

To serve, stir salad well and transfer to a serving bowl. Garnish with sliced eggs and reserved artichokes. Makes 8 to 10 servings.

Oil & Vinegar Dressing. Measure reserved **artichoke marinade** in a 1-quart glass measuring cup; add enough **olive oil** or salad oil to make ¾ cup *total*. Add ¾ cup **white wine vinegar;** 2 tablespoons chopped **parsley;** 3 large cloves **garlic,** minced or pressed; 2 tablespoons **lemon juice;** 1 tablespoon *each* **dry basil** and **ground coriander;** and 3 tablespoons **capers,** drained and chopped. Season with **salt** and **pepper** to taste. Mix until well blended.

Per serving: 315 calories, 9 grams protein, 26 grams carbohydrates, 21 grams total fat, 55 milligrams cholesterol, 1,018 milligrams sodium.

Black Bean & Potato Salad

Potato lovers will welcome this black bean-brightened salad for a casual supper. The potatoes are dressed while still warm—then served with ham and lettuce.

 2 pounds small thin-skinned potatoes
    (about 2 inches in diameter)
 2 tablespoons fermented black beans
 3 tablespoons white wine vinegar
 1 egg yolk
 1 clove garlic, minced or pressed
 ⅓ cup olive oil or salad oil
 ½ cup lightly packed coarsely chopped
    parsley
 ⅛ teaspoon freshly ground pepper
    Salt
    Butter lettuce leaves, washed and crisped
 6 to 8 thin slices Westphalian, Black Forest,
    or baked ham

Scrub potatoes; peel a band of skin around middle of each. In a 3- to 4-quart pan, cover potatoes with water and bring to a boil. Cover and boil gently until tender when pierced (about 30 minutes); drain well.

Rinse black beans in a wire strainer under cold running water; drain well and set aside.

In a large bowl, whisk vinegar, egg yolk, and garlic; slowly add oil, whisking until well blended. Stir in black beans, parsley, and pepper. Add warm potatoes and mix lightly until well coated. Season with salt to taste.

Mound potatoes in center of a platter. Pour any remaining dressing over potatoes. Surround with lettuce and ham. Makes 6 to 8 servings.

Per serving: 235 calories, 10 grams protein, 21 grams carbohydrates, 13 grams total fat, 51 milligrams cholesterol, 624 milligrams sodium.

Black Bean & Potato Salad
Slightly salty fermented black beans accent warm potatoes bathed in creamy vinaigrette. Add ham and lettuce leaves for a satisfying main-dish salad.

Seafood, Poultry & Meat Salads

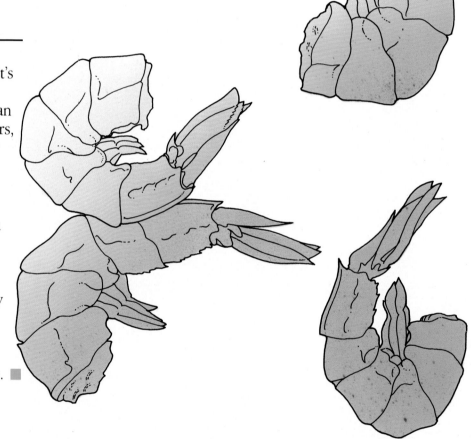

Just because it's a salad doesn't necessarily mean it's green and leafy. Seafood, poultry, and meat salads can become versatile appetizers, intriguing first courses, or entrées suitable for any season.

When it's too hot to cook, build a salad of such ingredients as shrimp or crab, cooked chicken or turkey, or roast beef from the delicatessen. Or, in any weather, prepare seafood, meat, or poultry in a sizzling hot stir-fry over a bed of cool, crisp lettuce. ■

Scallops, Sorrel & Orange Entrée Salad

Sorrel's lemony tang complements sweet orange slices and cold poached scallops in this elegant entrée salad.

    Poached Scallops (recipe follows)
4 **large oranges**
    Sorrel Dressing (recipe follows)
3 **cups loosely packed small tender sorrel leaves, washed and crisped**
    Salt
    Freshly ground black pepper

Prepare Poached Scallops; set aside.

Cut off peel and white membrane from oranges. Slice oranges crosswise into ½-inch-thick rounds. Prepare Sorrel Dressing.

On individual dinner plates, layer sorrel, oranges, and scallops; drizzle with dressing. Pass salt and pepper at the table. Makes 3 or 4 servings.

Poached Scallops. Rinse and drain 1½ pounds **scallops;** if large, cut into 1½-inch pieces. In a 3- to 4-quart pan, bring 1½ inches water to a boil over high heat. Add scallops and let water return to a boil. Reduce heat, cover, and simmer until scallops are just opaque in center (about 5 minutes); drain. Cover and refrigerate for 1½ hours or until next day.

Sorrel Dressing. In a food processor or blender, combine 2 tablespoons chopped tender **sorrel leaves** (discard coarse stems), 2 tablespoons *each* **white vinegar** and **water,** 1½ tablespoons chopped **fresh cilantro** (coriander), 2 teaspoons **dry mustard,** and 1 teaspoon **sugar.** Whirl until mixture is puréed. With motor running, pour in ½ cup **salad oil.** Whirl until well blended. Makes about ¾ cup.

Per serving: 497 calories, 31 grams protein, 28 grams carbohydrates, 29 grams total fat, 63 milligrams cholesterol, 276 milligrams sodium.

Shiny Noodles with Shrimp & Pork

Transparent noodles—bean threads—are bathed in a sweet-sour dressing, mingled with tiny shrimp and stir-fried pork, and spooned into lettuce leaves to eat. The idea comes from Thailand.

5 **to 6 ounces bean threads or 8 ounces spaghetti**
    Lime Dressing (recipe follows)
1 **tablespoon salad oil**
½ **pound ground pork**
1 **large clove garlic, minced or pressed**
½ **cup thinly sliced green onions**
¼ **pound small cooked shrimp**
2 **small heads red or green leaf lettuce (about 1 lb. *total*), washed and crisped**
    Lime wedges
    Sprigs of fresh cilantro (coriander)

In a large pan, bring 3 to 4 quarts water to a boil. Add noodles and cook until barely tender to bite (2 to 4 minutes for bean threads, about 9 minutes for spaghetti). Drain, rinse thoroughly, and drain again. Cut noodles into 8-inch-long strands.

Prepare Lime Dressing and set aside.

In an 8- to 10-inch frying pan, heat oil over medium-high heat. Add pork and garlic; cook, stirring, until pork is browned and crumbled. Discard fat. Stir in noodles, onions, shrimp, and dressing.

Arrange lettuce around edge of a large platter; mound noodle mixture in center. Garnish with lime and cilantro. To eat, spoon some of the noodle mixture into a lettuce leaf. Top with lime juice and cilantro; roll up to eat out of hand. Makes 3 main-dish servings or 8 to 10 appetizer servings.

Lime Dressing. Mix ½ cup **lime juice,** ¼ cup **sugar,** 2 to 3 tablespoons **fish sauce** or soy sauce, and ½ to ¾ teaspoon **crushed red pepper.**

Per serving: 576 calories, 33 grams protein, 84 grams carbohydrates, 12 grams total fat, 93 milligrams cholesterol, 1,430 milligrams sodium.

MEAT—CONVERTING POUNDS INTO CUPS

Many salad recipes call for cup measurements of bite-size cooked chicken, beef, ham, or turkey. If you don't have any leftovers, you can purchase meats just for the salads. Here's how to determine how much you'll need.

A 3-pound frying chicken will give you about 3 cups of meat. A chicken breast weighing about a pound will yield about 1½ cups of meat. And half a pound of cooked ham, beef, or turkey yields about 2 cups of meat. ■

California Shrimp Salad

To create this California classic, you marinate two celebrated West Coast ingredients—shrimp and avocado—in a piquant onion dressing.

- **2 pounds medium-size shrimp**
  Green Onion Dressing (recipe follows)
- **1 large ripe avocado**
- **1 large head iceberg lettuce, washed and crisped**

In a 4- to 5-quart pan, bring 1 quart water to a boil over high heat. Add shrimp, reduce heat, and simmer, uncovered, just until shrimp turn pink (4 to 6 minutes); do not overcook. Drain immediately and let cool slightly; then shell and devein.

Prepare Green Onion Dressing. Pit, peel, and cube avocado. Combine shrimp and avocado in a bowl. Pour dressing over mixture and turn gently until well coated. Cover and refrigerate for at least 1 hour or up to 2 hours.

Just before serving, cut lettuce into thin shreds; place on a serving platter or individual plates. With a slotted spoon, lift out shrimp-avocado mixture, reserving dressing, and mound on lettuce. Pass reserved dressing at the table. Makes 6 servings.

Per serving: 230 calories, 28 grams protein, 8 grams carbohydrates, 10 grams total fat, 174 milligrams cholesterol, 271 milligrams sodium.

Green Onion Dressing. Combine ¼ cup **olive oil** or salad oil, ¼ cup **white wine vinegar,** 2 tablespoons **lemon juice,** ½ teaspoon **garlic salt,** ⅛ teaspoon **seasoned pepper,** and ½ cup minced **green onions**. Mix until well blended.

Per tablespoon: 42 calories, .08 gram protein, .61 gram carbohydrates, 4 grams total fat, 0 milligram cholesterol, 78 milligrams sodium.

Classic Crab Louis

The origin of this famous crab salad remains a mystery, but we do know that Solari's Grill in San Francisco was one of the first restaurants to serve it, in 1911. It's made with fresh cracked crab.

- **2 large live or cooked Dungeness crabs in shell (4 to 5 lbs. *total*), or ¾ to 1 pound cooked crab meat**
  About 2 tablespoons salt
- **1 cup mayonnaise**
- **¼ cup tomato-based chili sauce**
- **¼ cup *each* finely chopped green bell pepper and green onions**
- **¼ cup whipping cream**
  Lemon juice
- **2 small heads iceberg lettuce, washed and crisped**
- **4 large firm-ripe tomatoes, cut into wedges**
- **4 hard-cooked eggs, cut into wedges**
  Parsley sprigs
  Lemon wedges

If you've purchased live crabs, plan to cook, crack, and clean them at least 2½ hours before serving. In a large kettle, bring about 8 quarts water to a boil over high heat; add 2 tablespoons of the salt. Grasp crabs from rear, firmly holding the last 1 or 2 legs on either side; drop into boiling water. Cover kettle and let water return to a boil. Then reduce heat and simmer for 20 minutes. Using tongs, lift out crabs; set aside until cool enough to handle.

To crack and clean cooked crab, grasp a front claw firmly and twist off, breaking it where claw joins crab's body. Repeat process with legs and remaining claw. Holding a leg or claw piece on its narrow edge on a cutting board, crack shell of each section with a mallet.

Pull off crab's broad back shell. Remove and discard gills and spongy parts under shell. Position a large, heavy knife down center of crab's body; tap back of knife with a mallet to cut body in half. Repeat to cut each half into 2 or 3 chunks, positioning knife between leg joints. Rinse all pieces well with cool water. Cover and refrigerate for at least 2 hours or up to 8 hours.

In a medium-size bowl, combine mayonnaise, chili sauce, bell pepper, and onions; mix until well blended. In another bowl, whip cream until stiff; fold into mayonnaise mixture. Season with salt and lemon juice to taste. If made ahead, cover and refrigerate for up to 2 hours.

Arrange 2 or 3 outer leaves of lettuce on individual plates; shred remaining lettuce and divide among plates. Remove meat from cracked crab pieces, reserving 4 to 8 legs for garnish. Shred crab meat and mound on lettuce. Arrange tomato and egg wedges around crab. Pour dressing over salads. Garnish with crab legs, parsley, and lemon. Makes 4 servings.

Per serving: 709 calories, 31 grams protein, 22 grams carbohydrates, 57 grams total fat, 437 milligrams cholesterol, 1,434 milligrams sodium.

California Shrimp Salad

Marinated shrimp co-star with mellow avocado, bold green onions, and shredded iceberg lettuce in this West Coast classic.

Red Chile Louis

To the venerable tradition of Louis salads, this Southwestern newcomer brings an appetizing fanfare of color and piquant flavor.

To cook, crack, and clean crabs, follow directions in Classic Crab Louis (page 34). Cover and refrigerate cracked crab pieces for at least 2 hours or up to 8 hours.

Prepare Red Chile Sauce. In a medium-size bowl, combine mayonnaise, lime juice, pepper, and ½ to ⅔ cup of the chile sauce. Mix until well blended; set dipping sauce aside.

Cut off peel and white membrane from oranges. Separate into segments. Thinly slice onion and separate into rings.

Line individual plates with lettuce. Arrange cracked crab pieces, orange segments, and onion rings on each plate. Garnish with cilantro and lime. Pass dipping sauce at the table. Makes 4 servings.

Per serving: 139 calories, 20 grams protein, 9 grams carbohydrates, 2 grams total fat, 113 milligrams cholesterol, 239 milligrams sodium.

Per tablespoon of dipping sauce: 43 calories, .20 gram protein, 1 gram carbohydrates, 4 grams total fat, 3 milligrams cholesterol, 32 milligrams sodium.

Red Chile Sauce. Rinse and pat dry 1 ounce dried whole **New Mexico or California chiles** (3 to 4 chiles). Place in a single layer on a baking sheet. Bake in a 450° oven just until chiles smell toasted (2 to 3 minutes). Let cool; break off and discard stems, and then shake out and discard seeds.

In a 1½- to 2-quart pan combine chiles, ¾ cup **water,** ⅓ cup chopped **onion,** and 1 small clove **garlic.** Cover and bring to a boil over high heat; then reduce heat and simmer until chiles are very soft when pierced (about 20 minutes). Remove from heat and let cool slightly.

Purée chile mixture in a blender until very smooth; or drain chile mixture, reserving liquid, and purée solids in a food processor, adding back liquid. Rub purée firmly through a wire strainer; discard residue. Season with **salt** to taste. If made ahead, cover and refrigerate for up to 1 week; freeze for longer storage. Makes ⅔ to ¾ cup.

Red Chile Louis

Called *ristras,* ropes of dried New Mexico chiles typically festoon kitchens of the Southwest and heat up the region's cooking. In this bold version of crab Louis, the same red chiles contribute to a potent dipping sauce.

> **2** **or 3 live or cooked Dungeness crabs in shell (4 to 5 lbs. *total*), or ¾ to 1 pound cooked crab meat**
> **Red Chile Sauce (recipe follows)**
> **½ cup mayonnaise**
> **2 tablespoons lime juice**
> **¼ to ½ teaspoon coarsely ground black pepper**
> **2 large oranges**
> **1 medium-size mild red onion**
> **Romaine lettuce leaves, washed and crisped**
> **Cilantro (coriander) sprigs**
> **Lime wedges**

Niçoise-style Fish Salad

A cold and colorful feast for the eye as
well as the palate, this Niçoise adaptation
offers poached fresh fish in lieu of the
usual tuna.

Niçoise-style Fish Salad

A popular French dish, Niçoise salad is most familiar
as a composition of tuna and vegetables. We've
chosen fresh poached or steamed red snapper—
or other firm-fleshed fish, such as cod, perch, or
turbot—to complete this classic.

4 to 6 small thin-skinned potatoes
    **Poached or Steamed Fish (recipe follows)
    or 2 cups flaked cooked fish**
½ pound thin green beans
    Vinaigrette Dressing (recipe follows)
    Red leaf lettuce, washed and crisped
**2 or 3 large firm-ripe tomatoes, cut into
    wedges**
3 or 4 hard-cooked eggs, cut into wedges
    Anchovy fillets (optional)
    Niçoise olives (optional)
    Chopped chives or green onions

Scrub potatoes; peel a band of skin around middle of
each potato. Arrange on a steamer rack and steam,
covered, over 1 inch of boiling water until tender
when pierced (25 to 30 minutes). Let cool to room
temperature.

Prepare Poached or Steamed Fish; set aside.

Meanwhile, remove ends and strings from beans.
Arrange on a steamer rack and steam, covered,
over 1 inch of boiling water just until tender-crisp
(5 to 8 minutes).

Prepare Vinaigrette Dressing. Place beans and
potatoes in a bowl, add ¼ cup of the dressing, and
mix lightly until well coated. In another bowl, combine flaked fish and remaining dressing; mix gently
until fish is well coated. Cover and refrigerate both
mixtures for at least 1 hour or up to 2 hours.

Line a large platter with lettuce. With a slotted
spoon, lift out vegetables and fish, reserving dressing, and arrange in separate mounds on lettuce.
Group tomato and egg wedges alongside; garnish

with anchovies and olives, if desired. Sprinkle fish
with chives. If made ahead, cover and refrigerate for
up to 3 hours. Pass reserved dressing at the table.
Makes 4 servings.

*Per serving: 356 calories, 31 grams protein, 43 grams
carbohydrates, 7 grams total fat, 331 milligrams cholesterol,
181 milligrams sodium.*

Poached or Steamed Fish. In a large pan, arrange
1 pound **fresh fish fillets** in 1 inch of simmering
water or place on a rack above 1 inch gently boiling
water. Cover and cook just until fish flakes easily
when prodded with a fork (allow about 10 minutes
for each inch of thickness). Drain, pat dry, and let
cool; separate into flakes.

Vinaigrette Dressing. Combine ⅓ cup **olive oil**
or salad oil, 2 tablespoons **red wine vinegar,** and
2 teaspoons *each* **Dijon mustard** and finely
chopped **red onion.** Mix until well blended.

*Per tablespoon: 81 calories, 0 gram protein, .37 gram
carbohydrates, 9 grams total fat, 0 milligram cholesterol,
38 milligrams sodium.*

Cool Chicken with Cumin & Citrus

Tart, juicy grapefruit, tangelo, and lime celebrate the succulence of steeped chicken topped with a light herbal-yogurt sauce. It's the perfect choice for a lazy spring or summer evening.

> **Steeped Chicken Breasts (recipe follows)**
> 1 *each* **pink grapefruit and lime**
> 1 **tangelo or 2 tangerines**
> **Spinach or romaine lettuce leaves, washed and crisped**
> **Cumin-Yogurt Sauce (recipe follows)**
> **Lime slice (optional)**

Prepare Steeped Chicken Breasts. Meanwhile, cut off peel and white membrane from grapefruit, lime, and tangelo. Cut between inner membranes and remove segments; place in a small bowl and set aside.

Without cutting all the way through, slice each chicken breast crosswise into ½-inch-thick sections. Line a serving platter with spinach leaves. Place chicken breasts on spinach and arrange citrus segments at each end of platter. (At this point, you may cover and refrigerate for up to 3 hours.)

Prepare Cumin-Yogurt Sauce. Spoon about 2 tablespoons of the sauce over each chicken breast. Garnish with lime slice, if desired. Pass remaining sauce at the table. Makes 4 servings.

Per serving: 152 calories, 22 grams protein, 13 grams carbohydrates, 2 grams total fat, 52 milligrams cholesterol, 71 milligrams sodium.

Steeped Chicken Breasts. Cut 2 small **whole chicken breasts** in half. In a wide 4- to 5-quart pan, bring 3 inches water to a rolling boil over high heat. Quickly immerse chicken in water. Remove pan from heat, cover tightly, and let steep for 15 minutes; do *not* uncover until time is up. Chicken is done when meat in thickest portion is no longer pink when slashed. Drain chicken and place in ice water until cool; drain again. Remove and discard skin and bones; pat dry.

Cumin-Yogurt Sauce. In a blender or food processor, combine ⅔ cup lightly packed **parsley sprigs,** ¾ cup **plain yogurt,** and 1 teaspoon **ground cumin.** Whirl until smooth. If made ahead, cover and refrigerate until next day. Makes about 1⅓ cups.

Per tablespoon: 6 calories, .47 gram protein, .74 gram carbohydrates, .14 gram total fat, .48 milligram cholesterol, 7 milligrams sodium.

Curried Chicken Salad with Papaya

Gingered curry dressing, papaya, and cashews entice you with the flavors of India. Complete this summertime salad with either chicken or turkey.

> **Curry Dressing (recipe follows)**
> 3 **cups diced cooked chicken or turkey**
> 1 **cup thinly sliced celery**
> ½ **cup thinly sliced green onions**
> **Salt and ground red pepper (cayenne)**
> **Large romaine lettuce leaves, washed and crisped**
> 2 **large ripe papayas, peeled, seeded, and sliced lengthwise**
> ¼ **cup salted roasted cashews**
> 1 **lemon, cut into quarters**

Prepare Curry Dressing. In a large bowl, combine chicken, celery, onions, and dressing; mix lightly until well coated. Season with salt and red pepper to taste.

Line individual dinner plates with lettuce. Mound chicken mixture on lettuce and arrange papaya slices alongside. Sprinkle with cashews and garnish with lemon quarters. Makes 4 servings.

Curry Dressing. Combine 1 cup **sour cream;** 2 tablespoons minced **candied ginger;** 1 tablespoon *each* **curry powder, lemon juice,** and **Dijon mustard;** and ½ teaspoon **cumin seeds.** Mix until well blended.

Per serving: 507 calories, 36 grams protein, 40 grams carbohydrates, 25 grams total fat, 119 milligrams cholesterol, 361 milligrams sodium.

Cool Chicken with Cumin & Citrus

Generous slices of steeped chicken, nestled on spinach and garnished with citrus, deliver a minimum of calories with a maximum of style.

MAIN-EVENT SALADS

Steak or chicken from the barbecue and a hearty salad are natural partners. So spectacular, though, are the following two salads that they'll upstage everything else on the menu.

Chunky Taco Salad

> **Chili Dressing (recipe follows)**
> 1 **flank steak (1½ to 2 lbs.)**
> 1 **can (7 oz.) green chile salsa**
> 1 **small head iceberg lettuce**
> ¼ **cup sliced green onions**
> 2 **cups coarsely crushed tortilla chips**
> 1 **can (15 oz.) kidney beans, drained**
> ½ **cup julienne strips Cheddar cheese**
> ½ **cup pitted ripe olive halves**
> 1 **tomato, cut into wedges**
> **Green lettuce leaves**
> 1 **ripe avocado**
> **Fresh cilantro (coriander) sprigs**

Prepare Chili Dressing. Pour ⅓ cup of the dressing over steak in a shallow baking dish; cover and let stand at room temperature for 2 hours (or cover and refrigerate for up to a day).

Add chile salsa to remaining dressing; set aside.

Cut lettuce into ¾-inch chunks; combine in a large salad bowl with onions and tortilla chips. Top with kidney beans, cheese, olives, and tomato. Tuck lettuce leaves around edges. (At this point, you may cover and refrigerate for up to 2 hours.)

Lift steak from marinade and place on a greased barbecue grill 4 to 6 inches above a solid bed of hot coals. Grill, turning once, until done to your liking when slashed (5 to 7 minutes on each side for medium-rare). Transfer to a serving platter. Pit, peel, and slice avocado; arrange on salad. Drizzle with

salsa mixture and garnish with cilantro. To serve steak, cut across the grain into thin, slanting slices. Makes 4 to 6 servings.

Chili Dressing. Mix ½ cup **salad oil**, ⅓ cup **red wine vinegar**, 1 teaspoon **chili powder**, ½ teaspoon **garlic salt**, and ⅛ teaspoon *each* **ground cumin** and crushed **red pepper.**

Per serving: 765 calories, 39 grams protein, 38 grams carbohydrates, 52 grams total fat, 90 milligrams cholesterol, 1,071 milligrams sodium.

Spanish Paella Salad

> 2 **cups water**
> ½ **teaspoon turmeric**
> 1 **cup long-grain white rice**
> **Pimento Dressing (recipe follows)**
> **Salt and pepper**
> 1 **frying chicken (3 to 3½ lbs.), quartered**
> **Garlic salt**
> 1 **jar (6 oz.) marinated artichoke hearts**
> 1 **tablespoon lemon juice**
> ¼ **teaspoon *each* dry rosemary and thyme leaves**
> 1 **cup thawed frozen peas**
> ½ **cup sliced pimento-stuffed olives**
> 1 **tomato, cut into wedges**

In a medium-size pan, combine water and turmeric. Bring to a boil over high heat. Add rice; reduce heat, cover, and simmer until rice is tender to bite (20 to 25 minutes).

Prepare Pimento Dressing. Spoon rice into a large bowl; add dressing and mix lightly. Season with salt and pepper to taste. Cover and refrigerate for at least 6 hours or until next day.

Sprinkle chicken with garlic salt. Drain artichoke hearts, reserving marinade. To marinade add lemon juice, rosemary, and thyme. Place chicken on a greased barbecue grill 4 to 6 inches above a solid bed of medium coals. Grill, turning and basting often with herb mixture, until meat near thighbone is no longer pink when slashed (40 to 45 minutes).

To rice mixture, add peas, olives, and artichoke hearts; mix lightly until well combined. Garnish with tomato and serve with chicken. Makes 4 servings.

Pimento Dressing. Mix ⅓ cup **salad oil**; 3 tablespoons **white vinegar**; 2 **green onions,** chopped; 2 tablespoons chopped **pimentos;** and 1 tablespoon **capers.**

Per serving: 944 calories, 54 grams protein, 50 grams carbohydrates, 56 grams total fat, 152 milligrams cholesterol, 728 milligrams sodium.

Hot & Cold Ginger Chicken Salad

Contrasts—hot versus cold, silken-textured versus crisp—tantalize the taste buds, as when hot and spicy chicken meets cool, crisp watercress.

- 3 **whole chicken breasts (3 to 3½ lbs. _total_), skinned and boned**
- **Ginger Marinade (recipe follows)**
- **About 6 tablespoons salad oil**
- 2 **large ripe avocados**
- 4 **tablespoons lemon juice**
- 3 **tablespoons olive oil or salad oil**
- 1½ **quarts lightly packed watercress sprigs (about 1 lb.), washed and crisped**
- **Salt and pepper**
- 1 **lemon, cut into 6 wedges**

Cut chicken breasts into pieces about ½ inch wide and 2 inches long. Prepare Ginger Marinade; add chicken and mix until well coated. Let stand at room temperature for 30 minutes, or cover and refrigerate until next day.

Lift chicken from marinade. Heat 2 tablespoons of the salad oil in a wok or wide frying pan over high heat. When oil is very hot, add chicken, a few pieces at a time—do not let pieces clump together. Cook, stirring, until lightly browned outside and white inside (2 to 3 minutes). With a slotted spoon, lift out chicken and set aside. Repeat with remaining chicken, adding remaining salad oil as needed. When all chicken has been cooked, set pan aside, reserving drippings.

Pit and peel avocados; cut lengthwise into thin wedges. Moisten with 1 tablespoon of the lemon juice; set aside.

In a large bowl, combine olive oil and remaining 3 tablespoons lemon juice; mix until well blended. Add watercress and season with salt and pepper to taste; mix lightly until well coated. Arrange watercress, avocado, and lemon wedges on individual dinner plates or on a serving platter.

Place pan with reserved drippings over high heat. Return chicken to pan and stir briefly just until heated through. Spoon hot chicken over watercress and serve immediately. Makes 6 servings.

Ginger Marinade. In a large bowl, mix 2 tablespoons **cornstarch** and ¼ cup **soy sauce** until smooth. Add ⅓ cup **sesame oil,** ⅓ cup minced **fresh ginger,** ¼ cup **lemon juice,** 1 tablespoon **salad oil,** ⅛ teaspoon hot **chili oil** or liquid hot pepper seasoning, and 1 clove **garlic,** minced or pressed. Mix until well blended.

Per serving: 596 calories, 44 grams protein, 12 grams carbohydrates, 43 grams total fat, 100 milligrams cholesterol, 639 milligrams sodium.

Strawberry Chicken Salad Plates

A lively fruit vinegar dressing enhances sliced chicken breasts. Strawberries and kiwi fruit add bright, sweet accents. _(Pictured on cover.)_

- **Steeped Chicken Breasts (see page 39)**
- **Fruit Vinegar Dressing (recipe follows)**
- **Butter lettuce leaves, washed and crisped**
- 2 **cups strawberries, halved**
- 2 **kiwi fruit, peeled and sliced**
- **Orange zest (optional)**
- **Slivered green onion tops (optional)**
- **Orange slices (optional)**

Prepare Steeped Chicken Breasts and Fruit Vinegar Dressing; set aside. (At this point, you may cover and refrigerate until next day.)

Line individual plates with lettuce leaves. Cut each chicken breast crosswise into ½-inch-thick slices. Reassemble each chicken breast in center of a plate, separating slices slightly. Arrange strawberries and kiwi slices beside chicken. Drizzle with some of the dressing, if desired. Garnish with orange zest, green onion tops, and orange slices, if desired. Pass remaining dressing at the table. Makes 4 servings.

Per serving: 143 calories, 21 grams protein, 11 grams carbohydrates, 2 grams total fat, 51 milligrams cholesterol, 60 milligrams sodium.

Fruit Vinegar Dressing. Combine ½ cup **salad oil;** ¼ cup **strawberry, raspberry, or cider vinegar;** 2 tablespoons **sugar;** ½ teaspoon _each_ **salt, paprika,** and **dry mustard;** and 1 finely chopped **green onion.** Mix until well blended.

Per tablespoon: 270 calories, .15 gram protein, 7 grams carbohydrates, 27 grams total fat, 0 milligram cholesterol, 274 milligrams sodium.

Winter Chicken Salad

Brightening a wintertime menu, sweet-tart marinated apricots embellish morsels of chicken in this main-dish salad. Pass around croissants or hot bran muffins.

⅓ cup *each* lemon juice and salad oil

2 tablespoons *each* poppy seeds, honey, and Dijon mustard

½ teaspoon grated lemon peel

½ cup moist-pack dried apricots

4 cups bite-size pieces cooked chicken breasts

⅓ cup chopped almonds

1 red apple

¼ cup sliced green onion tops
Salt
Butter lettuce leaves, washed and crisped

In a medium-size bowl, combine lemon juice, oil, poppy seeds, honey, mustard, and lemon peel; mix until well blended. Add apricots and stir; let stand for at least 30 minutes. Lift out apricots and set aside. Add chicken to dressing and mix lightly until well coated.

Spread almonds in a shallow baking pan and toast in a 350° oven until nuts are golden (about 8 minutes); set aside.

Just before serving, core apple and thinly slice; add to chicken with green onion tops and almonds. Mix lightly and season with salt to taste. Arrange lettuce on individual plates; mound chicken mixture on top. Surround with apricots. Makes 4 servings.

Per serving: 618 calories, 44 grams protein, 30 grams carbohydrates, 37 grams total fat, 125 milligrams cholesterol, 385 milligrams sodium.

Japanese Chicken Salad

If you like a salad with crunch, sample chicken with almonds, sesame seeds, and crackling pan-fried noodles from an Oriental soup mix package.

2 tablespoons salad oil

1 package (3 oz.) Oriental noodle soup mix

½ cup sliced almonds

2 tablespoons sesame seeds

2 cups diced or shredded cooked chicken breast

1 quart finely shredded green cabbage

½ cup chopped green onions
Salt
Rice Vinegar Dressing (recipe follows)

Heat oil in a wide frying pan over medium-high heat. Crumble noodles (do *not* use seasonings); add to oil with almonds and sesame seeds. Cook, stirring, until browned (3 to 4 minutes). Lift out mixture; drain. In a salad bowl, combine noodle mixture, chicken, cabbage, and onions; season with salt to taste. Prepare Rice Vinegar Dressing and pour over salad; mix lightly until well coated. Makes 6 servings.

Rice Vinegar Dressing. Mix ⅓ cup **salad oil,** ⅓ cup **rice vinegar** or distilled white vinegar, 5 teaspoons **sugar,** and ½ teaspoon **pepper.**

Per serving: 367 calories, 16 grams protein, 19 grams carbohydrates, 26 grams total fat, 32 milligrams cholesterol, 338 milligrams sodium.

Sesame Chicken Salad

Though Oriental cuisine doesn't include salads as we know them, many dishes such as this offer the same characteristics: they're fresh, light, and easy.

2 tablespoons sesame seeds

¼ cup salad oil

3 tablespoons lemon juice

1½ tablespoons *each* soy sauce and white wine vinegar

3 cloves garlic, minced or pressed

2 teaspoons finely minced fresh ginger

½ pound Chinese pea pods (also called snow or sugar peas)

½ pound bean sprouts

3 to 3½ cups shredded cooked chicken

Toast sesame seeds in a small frying pan over medium heat, shaking pan often, until seeds are golden (about 5 minutes). In a large bowl, mix seeds, oil, lemon juice, soy sauce, vinegar, garlic, and ginger until blended.

Fill a large pan halfway with water; bring to a boil. Add pea pods and bean sprouts; cook just until water boils. Drain, rinse with cold water, and drain again. Combine vegetables, chicken, and oil mixture and stir. Makes 4 servings.

Per serving: 432 calories, 40 grams protein, 11 grams carbohydrates, 25 grams total fat, 109 milligrams cholesterol, 613 milligrams sodium.

Sesame Chicken Salad

Inspired by Oriental cuisine, our salad of shredded chicken offers such appetizing accents as crisp pea pods and bean sprouts.

Cobb Salad

A classic example of salad artistry, Cobb Salad displays complementary colors, flavors, and textures in an appealing wheel of fresh ingredients.

Cook bacon over medium heat until crisp. Lift out, drain, and crumble; set aside. Pit, peel, and dice avocado; moisten with lemon juice and set aside.

Place lettuce in a large, wide salad bowl. In a medium-size bowl, combine vinegar, salt, garlic powder, pepper, chives, and oil; mix until well blended. Pour dressing over lettuce and mix lightly until well coated. Arrange lettuce in an even layer in bowl.

Place cheese in center of lettuce; surround with wedge-shaped sections of bacon, avocado, tomato, chicken, and eggs. Garnish with watercress, if desired. Serve immediately. Makes 4 servings.

Per serving: 776 calories, 36 grams protein, 13 grams carbohydrates, 66 grams total fat, 227 milligrams cholesterol, 1,183 milligrams sodium.

Cobb Salad

Hollywood has brightened our lives not only with famous movie stars but also with such celebrated culinary creations as the Cobb salad. Traditionally starring chicken, it's just as sensational when made with turkey, shrimp, or crabmeat.

- 1 **pound sliced bacon**
- 1 **large ripe avocado**
- 1 **tablespoon lemon juice**
- 1 **medium-size head iceberg lettuce, thinly shredded**
- 6 **tablespoons white wine vinegar**
- ½ **teaspoon salt**
- ⅛ **teaspoon *each* garlic powder and freshly ground pepper**
- 3 **tablespoons chopped chives**
- ½ **cup salad oil**
- ⅔ **cup (about 3 oz.) finely crumbled blue-veined cheese**
- 1 **large tomato, seeded and chopped**
- 1½ **cups diced cooked chicken**
- 2 **hard-cooked eggs, chopped**
  Watercress sprigs (optional)

Coriander Chicken Salad

Hot and pungent, spicy and sweet—all these words describe *so see gai,* an out-of-the-ordinary chicken salad. It's a Chinese restaurant favorite that's easy to duplicate at home.

- 1 **frying chicken (3 to 3½ lbs.)**
- 2 **tablespoons soy sauce**
  Mustard Dressing (recipe follows)
- ¼ **cup sesame seeds**
- 1¼ **to 1½ quarts shredded iceberg lettuce**
- ¼ **cup *each* chopped fresh cilantro (coriander) and sliced green onions**

Rinse chicken and pat dry. Place soy sauce in a deep bowl; add chicken and turn to coat. Cover and refrigerate, turning often, for at least 2 hours or until next day.

Lift chicken from bowl and place, breast side up, on a rack in a roasting pan. Roast in a 425° oven until skin is crisp and browned and meat near thighbone

Coriander Chicken Salad

A zesty Chinese specialty that often appears on restaurant banquet menus, this salad also serves as a tempting entrée on its own at home.

is no longer pink when slashed (about 45 minutes). Let cool on rack.

Strip meat, with skin attached, from bones; cut into ¼-inch slivers. (At this point, you may cover and refrigerate until next day.)

Prepare Mustard Dressing and set aside. Toast sesame seeds in a wide frying pan over medium heat, shaking pan often, until seeds are golden (about 2 minutes).

Just before serving, arrange lettuce in a ½-inch-thick bed on a large platter. In a large bowl, combine chicken, sesame seeds, cilantro, onions, and dressing. Mix, lifting with 2 forks, until well blended. Mound chicken mixture on lettuce. Makes about 4 servings.

Mustard Dressing. Combine 1 tablespoon *each* **dry mustard** and **water**; stir until well blended. Add ¼ cup *each* **sesame oil** and **salad oil**, 2 tablespoons **lemon juice**, 4 teaspoons *each* **sugar** and **soy sauce**, and 1 teaspoon **Chinese five-spice** or ½ teaspoon ground cinnamon. Mix until well blended.

Per serving: 754 calories, 51 grams protein, 12 grams carbohydrates, 56 grams total fat, 154 milligrams cholesterol, 933 milligrams sodium.

Turkey Romaine Salad

Reserve a cup of packaged herb-seasoned croutons from your holiday stuffing preparations to scatter over this refreshingly crisp salad. Or make your own delicious, buttery ones.

- ⅓ **cup slivered almonds**
- 1 **large head romaine lettuce, washed and crisped**
- 3 **cups cubed cooked turkey or chicken**
- 3 **tablespoons grated Parmesan cheese**
- ½ **cup sliced water chestnuts**

1 **cup croutons, purchased or homemade (see page 55)**
Nippy Vinaigrette Dressing (recipe follows)

Spread almonds in a shallow baking pan and toast in a 350° oven until nuts are golden (about 8 minutes); set aside.

Tear lettuce into bite-size pieces. In a salad bowl, combine lettuce, turkey, cheese, water chestnuts, croutons, and almonds. Prepare Nippy Vinaigrette Dressing and pour over salad. Mix lightly until well coated. Serve immediately. Makes 6 to 8 servings.

Nippy Vinaigrette Dressing. Combine ¼ cup *each* **salad oil** and **olive oil** (or all salad oil), 3 tablespoons **white wine vinegar**, 1 teaspoon *each* **dry mustard** and **lemon juice**, ½ teaspoon **Worcestershire**, ¼ teaspoon *each* **salt** and **liquid hot pepper seasoning**, and a dash of **pepper**. Mix until well blended.

Per serving: 392 calories, 22 grams protein, 25 grams carbohydrates, 23 grams total fat, 42 milligrams cholesterol, 414 milligrams sodium.

Taco Salad

A hot, chili-flavored topping of ground beef and red beans on a crisp base of shredded lettuce makes a whole-meal salad reminiscent of a tostada.

    Guacamole (recipe follows)
1 pound lean ground beef
1 medium-size onion, finely chopped
1 can (15 oz.) kidney beans, drained
1½ teaspoons chili powder
½ teaspoon ground cumin
½ cup catsup or tomato sauce
1 medium-size ripe avocado
1 medium-size head iceberg lettuce, shredded
1 cup (4 oz.) shredded Cheddar or jack cheese
2 medium-size firm-ripe tomatoes, cut into wedges
3 hard-cooked eggs, cut into wedges
    Tortilla chips
    Sour cream
    Red onion rings
    Sliced ripe olives
    Chopped green onions (including tops)
    Green peperoncini (optional)
    Lime wedges (optional)

Prepare Guacamole; set aside.

Crumble beef into a wide frying pan and add onion. Cook, stirring, over medium-high heat until meat is no longer pink and onion is limp; discard drippings. Stir in kidney beans, chili powder, cumin, and catsup; simmer over low heat for about 5 minutes.

Pit, peel, and slice avocado. Arrange lettuce on individual plates. Layer beef mixture, cheese, guacamole, tomatoes, eggs, and avocado on lettuce. Surround with tortilla chips. Top with sour cream, onion rings, olives, and a sprinkling of green onions. Garnish with peperoncini and lime wedges, if desired. Makes 4 servings.

Guacamole. Cut 1 large ripe **avocado** in half; remove pit and scoop out flesh. In a medium-size bowl, coarsely mash avocado with a fork. Add 1 small clove **garlic,** minced or pressed; 1½ tablespoons **lime or lemon juice;** ¼ teaspoon **salt;** a few drops **liquid hot pepper seasoning;** and 1 tablespoon minced fresh **cilantro** (coriander). Mix until well blended. If made ahead, cover and refrigerate for up to 3 hours.

Per serving: 786 calories, 43 grams protein, 46 grams carbohydrates, 50 grams total fat, 304 milligrams cholesterol, 1,177 milligrams sodium.

Hot & Sour Beef with Cucumber

This refreshing cold beef salad from Thailand is served atop butter lettuce leaves. You can offer forks; or use the lettuce as a wrapper to enclose the salad and eat it burrito-style.

1 pound boneless beef sirloin steak, about 1¼ inches thick
1 medium-size cucumber, peeled
¼ cup *each* lime juice and thinly sliced red onion
2 tablespoons fish sauce or soy sauce
¼ to ½ teaspoon ground red pepper (cayenne)
½ teaspoon sesame oil (optional)
    Butter lettuce leaves, washed and crisped
1 teaspoon sesame seeds
    Fresh mint or cilantro (coriander) sprigs

Slash fat edge of steak at 2-inch intervals. Place on a rack in a broiler pan and broil 3 inches from heat, turning once, until well browned on outside and pink inside (about 12 minutes *total*).

Meanwhile, cut cucumber in half lengthwise; scoop out and discard seeds. Thinly slice cucumber into crescents.

Slice steak across the grain into thin bite-size strips. In a large bowl, combine cucumber, steak, lime juice, onion, fish sauce, red pepper, and, if desired, sesame oil. Mix lightly until well coated. Cover and refrigerate for at least 1 hour or up to 6 hours.

Arrange lettuce on a serving platter. Mound beef mixture on lettuce and garnish with sesame seeds and mint sprigs. Makes 3 or 4 servings.

Per serving: 301 calories, 22 grams protein, 5 grams carbohydrates, 22 grams total fat, 72 milligrams cholesterol, 719 milligrams sodium.

Taco Salad

If you love the experience of attacking a taco, you're sure to delight in this high-protein salad, which serves the same fiesta of flavors with a little more decorum.

GRAND SALAD BUFFET

At your next buffet, set up our sensational salad bar. From ingredients you can easily prepare in advance, up to two dozen guests can create their own entrée salads.

>   2 **frying chickens (about 3½ lbs. *each*)**
>   1 **canned ham (3 lbs.)**
>   1 **to 1½ pounds *each* Swiss and sharp Cheddar cheese**
>   1 **large cauliflower**
>   2 **large heads *each* iceberg, romaine, and red leaf lettuce, washed and crisped**
>   2 **large red onions, thinly sliced**
>   1 **pound carrots, thinly sliced**
>   3 **or 4 large zucchini, thinly sliced**
>   4 **cucumbers, peeled and sliced**
> 1½ **pounds mushrooms, quartered**
>   2 **baskets cherry tomatoes**
>   1 **basket alfalfa sprouts**
>   1 **small head red cabbage, shredded**
>   4 **cups Creamy Tarragon Vinaigrette (page 85)**

Place chickens and ham on a rack in a roasting pan. Bake, uncovered, in a 350° oven until meat near thighbone is no longer pink when slashed (about 1½ hours).

Let chicken cool; tear meat into thin strips discarding skin and bones. Cut ham and cheeses into thin strips. Cover and refrigerate for up to 2 days.

Slice cauliflower flowerets ¼ inch thick. Tear lettuce into bite-size pieces. Refrigerate cauliflower, lettuce, onions, carrots, zucchini, cucumbers, mushrooms, tomatoes, sprouts, and cabbage for up to a day.

Prepare Creamy Tarragon Vinaigrette.

To serve, combine lettuce and cabbage in a large bowl. Arrange meats, cheeses, vegetables, and dressing separately as desired. Makes about 24 servings. ▪

Korean Beef Salad

As an extra convenience, you can make this attractive salad ahead of time. Mix in its spicy dressing at the table just before serving.

> 1½ **pounds boneless beef top round, ½ to ¾ inch thick**
>   2 **tablespoons soy sauce**
>   2 **teaspoons *each* sugar and sherry**
>   **About 4 tablespoons salad oil**
>   4 **green onions, thinly sliced**
>   1 **small head iceberg lettuce, shredded**
>   2 **small onions, thinly sliced**
>   1 **basket cherry tomatoes, halved**
>   ½ **pound mushrooms, sliced**
>   **Spicy Chili Dressing (recipe follows)**

Partially freeze beef so it will be easier to slice. Cut beef across the grain into 1½-inch-long strips about ⅛ inch thick. In a medium-size bowl, combine soy sauce, sugar, and sherry. Mix in beef; let stand, stirring once, for at least 30 minutes or up to 1 hour.

Heat 2 tablespoons of the oil in a wide frying pan over high heat. When oil is hot, add a third of the beef strips. Cook, stirring, just until meat is no longer pink (about 1 minute); remove from pan. Repeat with remaining beef, adding more oil as needed. Combine beef with green onions and set aside.

Spread lettuce in a large shallow bowl. Arrange beef, sliced onions, tomatoes, and mushrooms on lettuce. Cover and refrigerate for at least 1 hour or up to 10 hours.

Prepare Spicy Chili Dressing; drizzle over salad and mix lightly until well coated. Serve immediately. Makes 6 to 8 servings.

Spicy Chili Dressing. Combine ⅓ cup **soy sauce;** ½ cup **white wine vinegar;** 2 cloves **garlic,** minced or pressed; 1½ teaspoons minced **fresh ginger;** 1 teaspoon **chili oil** or ¼ teaspoon ground red pepper (cayenne); and 2 teaspoons **sesame oil.** Mix until well blended.

Per serving: 260 calories, 21 grams protein, 8 grams carbohydrates, 16 grams total fat, 51 milligrams cholesterol, 1,096 milligrams sodium.

Roast Pork & Papaya Salad

Proving deliciously that almost anything goes in salad-making, baked pork stew combines with lettuce and papaya in a salad version of curry. We've even scattered raisins and almonds on top.

Yogurt Dressing (recipe follows)
2 **pounds boneless pork butt or shoulder,** trimmed of fat and cut into ½-inch cubes
2 **cloves garlic, minced or pressed**
1 **teaspoon cumin seeds**
1½ **teaspoons curry powder**
¼ **teaspoon crushed red pepper**
1 **tablespoon salad oil**
½ **cup sliced almonds**
½ **cup raisins**
2 **quarts butter lettuce leaves, washed and** crisped
1 **large ripe papaya, peeled, seeded, and** thinly sliced
Salt and pepper

Prepare Yogurt Dressing and set aside.

In a large bowl, combine pork, garlic, cumin seeds, curry powder, and crushed red pepper. Spread in a shallow rimmed 10- by 15-inch baking pan. Bake, uncovered, in a 475° oven, stirring often, until meat is very well browned (about 25 minutes).

With a slotted spoon, transfer pork to a bowl and keep warm. Heat oil in a wide frying pan over medium-high heat. Add almonds and cook, stirring, until nuts are lightly browned (1 to 2 minutes). With a slotted spoon, lift nuts out and drain on paper towels. Add raisins to pan and cook, stirring, until puffy; remove pan from heat.

Line individual plates with lettuce. Mound pork on lettuce and arrange papaya slices alongside. Spoon dressing over salads and sprinkle with almonds and raisins. Pass salt and pepper at the table. Makes 4 to 6 servings.

Yogurt Dressing. Combine 2 cups **plain yogurt,** 1½ tablespoons **mustard seeds,** ¾ cup chopped **cilantro** (coriander), ¾ cup finely chopped **green onions,** and 1 teaspoon **cumin seeds;** mix until well blended. Season with **salt** to taste. If made ahead, cover and refrigerate for up to 2 days.

Per serving: 411 calories, 31 grams protein, 28 grams carbohydrates, 21 grams total fat, 76 milligrams cholesterol, 120 milligrams sodium.

Piquant Pork & Potato Salad Platter

In a salad that will satisfy any appetite, a mustard-based dressing, seasoned two ways, accompanies both potatoes and roast pork.

1 **pound thin-skinned potatoes**
½ **cup** *each* **salad oil and vinegar**
2 **teaspoons Dijon mustard**
3 **green onions, chopped**
2 **tablespoons minced dill pickle**
3 **tablespoons chopped parsley**
Salt and pepper
1 **tablespoon** *each* **minced shallot and** drained capers
1 **pound thinly sliced roast pork or turkey**
Red lettuce leaves, washed and crisped
1 **jar (7 oz.) roasted red peppers**

Scrub potatoes (do not peel). Place in a 3-quart pan with about 1 inch water. Cover and boil gently until potatoes are tender when pierced (about 30 minutes). When cool enough to handle, peel and cut into ¾-inch cubes; place in a large bowl and set aside.

In a medium-size bowl, combine oil, vinegar, and mustard; mix until well blended. Pour half the oil mixture into another bowl, reserving remaining mixture, and stir in onions, pickle, and parsley; pour over potatoes and mix lightly until well coated. Season with salt and pepper to taste. Set potatoes aside for at least 1 hour.

To remaining dressing, add shallot and capers; mix until well blended. Stir in meat, turning until well coated. Season with salt and pepper to taste. (At this point, you may cover and refrigerate both mixtures until next day; let come to room temperature before serving.)

Line a serving platter with lettuce. Overlap pork slices at one end, spooning any remaining dressing over meat. Mound potatoes at opposite end. Cut peppers lengthwise into wide strips and arrange in center. Makes 4 servings.

Per serving: 635 calories, 35 grams protein, 26 grams carbohydrates, 43 grams total fat, 90 milligrams cholesterol, 305 milligrams sodium.

Oriental Meatball Salad

Hot, gingery meatballs nestle on a bed of cold lettuce in an appealing main-dish salad. Baking, rather than sautéing the meatballs, makes for easier preparation.

Beef Meatballs with Red Ginger (recipe follows)
- 1 **teaspoon sugar**
- 1 **tablespoon cornstarch**
- 1 **tablespoon mirin (sweet rice wine) or sherry**
- 2 **teaspoons soy sauce**
- ½ **teaspoon vinegar**
- 1½ **cups water**
- 1 **beef bouillon cube**
- 1 **head iceberg lettuce, very finely shredded**
- ¼ **cup thinly sliced green onions**
- 1 **lemon, cut into wedges**

Prepare Beef Meatballs with Red Ginger. Meanwhile, combine sugar and cornstarch in a small pan; add mirin, soy sauce, vinegar, and water; stir until smooth. Add bouillon cube and cook over medium heat, stirring constantly, until bouillon cube is dissolved and mixture boils and thickens; keep warm.

Arrange lettuce on a serving platter. Spoon hot meatballs on lettuce; sprinkle with onions and garnish with lemon. Serve immediately. Pass sauce at the table. Makes 4 servings.

Beef Meatballs with Red Ginger. In a large bowl, combine 1 pound **lean ground beef;** 1 medium-size **onion,** very finely chopped; 1 clove **garlic,** minced or pressed; 4 teaspoons finely chopped **pickled red ginger;** ¼ teaspoon **salt;** dash of **pepper;** and, if desired, 1 teaspoon **sesame oil.** Mix until well blended; cover, and refrigerate for 1 hour.

Shape mixture into 1-inch balls. Place about 1½ inches apart on greased shallow rimmed baking sheets. Bake, uncovered, in a 450° oven until browned (10 to 12 minutes).

Per serving: 292 calories, 23 grams protein, 13 grams carbohydrates, 17 grams total fat, 66 milligrams cholesterol, 628 milligrams sodium.

Orange Aïoli & Roast Beef Salad

Assemble your own salad from an assortment of vegetables and strips of roasted meat. The dressing is an orange-infused garlic mayonnaise.

Orange Aïoli (recipe follows)
- 2 **cups slivered or torn bite-size pieces boneless roast beef, pork, lamb, or turkey**
- 1 **to 2 cups diagonally sliced fennel or celery**
- 1 **can (15 oz.) white kidney beans (cannellini), drained**
- 8 **to 12 small romaine lettuce leaves, washed and crisped**
- 1 **bunch radishes**
- 1 **small orange, cut into quarters (optional)**
- **Italian parsley sprigs (optional)**

Prepare Orange Aïoli; spoon into a small bowl and place on a large serving platter. Surround with separate mounds of meat, fennel, kidney beans, lettuce, and radishes. Garnish with orange quarters and parsley, if desired.

Top individual servings with aïoli and squeeze on orange juice, if desired. Makes 4 servings.

Per serving: 167 calories, 17 grams protein, 16 grams carbohydrates, 4 grams total fat, 32 milligrams cholesterol, 368 milligrams sodium.

Orange Aïoli. Combine ½ cup **mayonnaise;** 4 large cloves **garlic,** minced or pressed; 1 teaspoon grated **orange rind;** and 3 tablespoons **orange juice.** Mix until well blended. If made ahead, cover and refrigerate for up to 2 days.

Per tablespoon: 76 calories, .22 gram protein, 1 gram carbohydrates, 8 grams total fat, 6 milligrams cholesterol, 57 milligrams sodium.

Orange Aïoli & Roast Beef Salad

As a dip or a drizzle, our intense garlic-and-orange aïoli makes adventurous dining of crisp vegetables and strips of beef.

Garlic Frankfurter Dinner Salad

This quick supper salad mingles the unusual and savory flavors of sliced garlic sausage and spicy kuminost cheese.

Peel and discard skins from sausages; cut meat into diagonal ¼-inch slices. Add to dressing. Cut cheese into thin matchstick pieces; add to sausage mixture and stir gently until well coated. Cover and let stand at room temperature for at least 30 minutes or up to 2 hours. If made ahead, cover and refrigerate for up to 2 days; let come to room temperature before serving.

Line individual plates or a salad bowl with lettuce and top with cabbage. Spoon sausage mixture on greens. Garnish with tomatoes, if desired. Makes 4 servings.

Per serving: 582 calories, 19 grams protein, 7 grams carbohydrates, 53 grams total fat, 75 milligrams cholesterol, 1,728 milligrams sodium.

Garlic Frankfurter Dinner Salad

When it's too hot to cook, make salad. Better yet, in a few easy minutes, produce a cheese-and-sausage supper salad. There's sweet pickle relish in the dressing, so all you need add is rye bread.

> ¼ **cup salad oil**
> 1 **tablespoon white wine vinegar**
> 2 **green onions, chopped**
> 1 **tablespoon sweet pickle relish, drained**
> 1 **teaspoon Dijon mustard**
> ½ **teaspoon salt**
> ¼ **teaspoon pepper**
> 1 **pound fully cooked garlic frankfurters**
> 3 **ounces kuminost cheese**
>   **Green leaf lettuce, washed and crisped**
>   **About 2 cups shredded red cabbage**
>   **Tomato wedges (optional)**

In a large bowl, combine oil, vinegar, onions, relish, mustard, salt, and pepper; mix until well blended.

Hot Potato & Wurst Salad

Frothy steins of beer are the obvious complement to this hot potato salad with sliced knackwurst and bratwurst.

> 2½ **pounds medium-size thin-skinned potatoes**
> 2 *each* **large knackwurst (about 10 oz. *total*) and large bratwurst (about 12 oz. *total*)**
> 1 **tablespoon salad oil**
> 4 **teaspoons *each* all-purpose flour and sugar**
> 1 **teaspoon *each* salt, dry mustard, and celery seeds**
> ⅔ **cup regular-strength chicken broth**
> ⅓ **cup white wine vinegar**
> ¼ **cup finely chopped parsley**
> 1 **small red onion, sliced and separated into rings**
> ½ **cup sliced celery**

Hot Potato & Wurst Salad

True to the German tradition, this hot bratwurst- and knockwurst-laden potato salad offers robust and zesty flavors.

Scrub potatoes (do not peel). Place in a 3-quart pan with about 1 inch water. Cover and boil gently until potatoes are just tender when pierced (about 30 minutes). Drain and set aside. When cool enough to handle, peel and slice potatoes about ¼ inch thick.

Meanwhile, peel and discard casings from sausages; cut meat into diagonal ¼-inch slices. Heat oil in a wide frying pan over medium heat. Add sausages and cook, stirring often, until lightly browned. Remove meat from pan and set aside, reserving drippings.

Add flour, sugar, salt, mustard, and celery seeds to pan. Cook, stirring, until mixture is hot and bubbly. Gradually stir in broth and vinegar; cook, stirring, until dressing boils and thickens. Add potatoes, meat, parsley, onion, and celery; stir gently until heated through. Serve immediately. Makes 6 servings.

Per serving: 515 calories, 18 grams protein, 42 grams carbohydrates, 30 grams total fat, 61 milligrams cholesterol, 1,296 milligrams sodium.

Sausage & Potato Vinaigrette

Sliced whole potatoes and plump garlic sausages share a creamy vinaigrette dressing to make a simple, hearty meal. Use a fully cooked sausage that only needs reheating; if the special French garlic salami isn't available, you can substitute Polish sausage (kielbasa) or knackwurst.

> 3½ **pounds large russet potatoes**
> 1 **egg yolk**
> 1 **teaspoon Dijon mustard**
> ¼ **cup white wine vinegar**
> 1 **cup olive oil or salad oil**
> ¼ **teaspoon dry tarragon**
> 2 **green onions, chopped**
> 1 **tablespoon chopped parsley**

> 1 **clove garlic, minced or pressed**
> **Sugar**
> **Salt and pepper**
> 1½ **pounds French garlic salami, kielbasa, or garlic knackwurst**

Scrub potatoes (do not peel). Place in a large pan with about 1 inch water. Cover and boil gently until potatoes are tender when pierced (about 30 minutes). Drain and place on a warm serving platter.

Meanwhile, in a medium-size bowl, combine egg yolk, mustard, and vinegar; whisk until blended. Slowly add oil in a thin, steady stream, whisking until dressing thickens. Stir in tarragon, onions, parsley, and garlic. Add a pinch of sugar and season with salt and pepper to taste.

In a wide frying pan, bring about 1 inch water to a gentle simmer over medium heat. Add salami, cover, and simmer gently until heated through (about 7 minutes); do not boil. Drain, remove casings if necessary, and cut into ¼-inch slices; keep warm.

Cut potatoes crosswise into ¼-inch slices, keeping potato shape intact. Pour half the dressing over potatoes and top with hot sausage. Pour remaining dressing over all. Serve hot. Makes 4 to 6 servings.

Per serving: 914 calories, 22 grams protein, 51 grams carbohydrates, 70 grams total fat, 125 milligrams cholesterol, 1,061 milligrams sodium.

Spiced Beef & Rice Stick Salad

Crisp fresh bean sprouts and thin rice noodles contrast pleasantly with piquant stir-fried beef in a salad of Oriental tradition.

        8 ounces dry rice sticks
           (rice noodles or *mai fun*)
        1 cup thinly sliced radishes
        2 tablespoons salt
        6 tablespoons white wine vinegar
       ¼   cup sugar
        4 tablespoons fish sauce or soy sauce
       ½   teaspoon crushed red pepper
       ½   pound bean sprouts, rinsed and drained
        1 cup fresh mint leaves
       ¼   cup salad oil
       1½ pounds beef sirloin steak, trimmed of fat
           and thinly sliced
        8 to 10 large cloves garlic, minced or
           pressed
       ¼   cup sliced green onions
       ½   cup coarsely chopped roasted peanuts
           Lime wedges

Place rice sticks in a large bowl; pour boiling water over to cover noodles. Let stand until tender to bite (about 30 minutes); drain well and set aside.

Meanwhile, combine radishes, salt, and 4 tablespoons of the vinegar. Let stand until radishes are limp (about 30 minutes). Drain radishes, rinse well under cold running water, and drain again; set aside.

In a wok or wide frying pan, combine remaining 2 tablespoons vinegar, sugar, 2 tablespoons of the fish sauce, and ¼ teaspoon of the crushed red pepper. Bring to a boil over high heat, stirring until sugar is dissolved. Pour over noodles and add radishes; mix lightly until well coated.

Mound noodle mixture on one side of a large platter or on individual plates. Arrange bean sprouts on other side. Garnish with mint leaves.

Place wok or frying pan over high heat. When pan is hot, add oil; then add steak slices, garlic,

remaining 2 tablespoons fish sauce, and remaining ¼ teaspoon crushed red pepper. Cook, stirring, until meat is no longer pink (3 to 4 minutes). Remove from heat and stir in onions.

Spoon meat mixture over noodles and bean sprouts; serve immediately. Pass peanuts and lime wedges at the table. Makes 4 to 6 servings.

Per serving: 494 calories, 25 grams protein, 49 grams carbohydrates, 22 grams total fat, 52 milligrams cholesterol, 1,367 milligrams sodium.

HOMEMADE CROUTONS

Once you've tasted these crunchy seasoned croutons, you'll never throw out day-old French bread again.

Seasoned Croutons. Cut about ½ pound day-old **French bread** into ½-inch cubes (you should have about 3 cups). Spread evenly on a rimmed baking sheet. Bake in a 300° oven for 10 minutes. Remove from oven and set aside; reduce oven temperature to 275°.

In a wide frying pan, melt ¼ cup **butter** or margarine over medium heat; or heat ¼ cup olive oil or salad oil. Remove from heat and stir in 2 or 3 of the following: 1 teaspoon **herbes de Provence** or Italian herb seasoning (or ¼ teaspoon *each* dry basil and oregano, thyme, and marjoram leaves); ½ teaspoon **Worcestershire**; 1 tablespoon grated **Parmesan cheese**; 1 clove **garlic**, minced or pressed.

Add toasted bread cubes, mixing lightly until evenly coated. Spread on baking sheet and bake until crisp and lightly browned (about 30 more minutes). Let cool. Store in a covered container at room temperature for up to a week or freeze for up to a month. Makes about 3 cups. ■

Spiced Beef & Rice Stick Salad

Fired with chiles, then cooled with mint, a salad of Oriental stir-fried beef and bean sprouts intrigues with contrasting flavors and temperatures.

Pasta & Rice Salads

Pasta and rice salads have gained much sophistication of late. Such salads now boast a variety of fresh ingredients, creating intriguing combinations to please even the most particular palate.

Many of our salads, such as Tabbuli and Sushi Salad, derive their unique flavors from their foreign heritage. Some are hearty enough to make a meal; others, like Pasta & Pepper Salad, play a supporting role alongside meat or chicken.

Whichever salad you choose, prepare it ahead of time so its flavors have time to blend. ▪

Condiment Macaroni Salad

Begin with a basic macaroni salad and add a selection of savory condiments. The result: hearty salads to suit every taste. And everything can be prepared in advance.

1 pound **salad macaroni or other small-size dry pasta**
12 **green onions,** sliced
1 cup thinly sliced **celery**
1 jar (4 oz.) **diced pimentos,** drained
1½ cups **mayonnaise**
3 tablespoons **dill pickle liquid or vinegar**
2 tablespoons *each* **prepared horseradish and mustard**
Salt and pepper
Lettuce leaves, washed and crisped
Cherry tomato halves
Condiments (suggestions follow)

In a large pan, bring 6 quarts water to a boil over high heat. Add pasta; let water return to a boil and cook, uncovered, just until tender to bite (about 10 minutes). Or cook according to package directions. Drain, rinse with cold water, and drain well again. Place pasta in a large bowl and add onions, celery, and pimentos.

In a small bowl, combine mayonnaise, pickle liquid, horseradish, and mustard; mix until well blended. Add to pasta mixture and stir lightly until well coated. Season with salt and pepper to taste. Cover and refrigerate for at least 4 hours or until next day.

Line a large shallow bowl with lettuce. Mound pasta salad on lettuce and surround with tomatoes. Place condiments of your choice in bowls to add to individual servings as desired. Makes 6 to 8 servings.

Per serving: 522 calories, 8 grams protein, 47 grams carbohydrates, 34 grams total fat, 24 milligrams cholesterol, 322 milligrams sodium.

Condiments. Serve 4 or 5 of the following: 1½ to 2 cups *each* chopped **dill pickles,** cubed **sharp Cheddar cheese,** sliced or chopped **hard-cooked eggs,** small **cooked shrimp,** diced **cooked chicken** or **turkey,** drained flaked **tuna.**

Tuna & Fruit Salad

What makes extraordinary eating of ordinary tuna-pasta salad? Discover the answer as you savor what we've added—a mustardy-curry dressing and morsels of fresh fruit.

⅓ cup **sliced almonds**
½ cup **small shell macaroni**
1 large **apple**
2½ tablespoons **lemon juice**
1 cup sliced **celery**
½ cup **halved seeded grapes**
¼ cup thinly sliced **green onions**
1 can (6½ oz.) **tuna,** drained
½ cup **mayonnaise**
1 teaspoon **Dijon mustard**
1½ teaspoons **curry powder**
Salt
Lettuce leaves, washed and crisped

Spread almonds in a shallow baking pan; toast in a 350° oven until golden (about 8 minutes); set aside.

In a 5- to 6-quart pan, bring 2 quarts water to a boil over high heat. Add pasta; let water return to a boil and cook, uncovered, just until tender to bite (about 10 minutes). Or cook according to package directions. Drain, rinse with cold water, and drain well again.

Meanwhile, peel apple, if desired; core and dice. Place in a large bowl and moisten with lemon juice; add celery, grapes, onions, and pasta. Break tuna into bite-size pieces and add to pasta mixture.

In a small bowl, combine mayonnaise, mustard, and curry powder; mix until well blended. Spoon dressing over pasta mixture and mix lightly until well coated. Season with salt to taste. (At this point, you may cover and refrigerate for up to 2 hours.)

Just before serving, stir in half the almonds. Line a serving bowl or individual plates with lettuce. Mound pasta mixture on lettuce and sprinkle with remaining almonds. Makes 2 servings.

Per serving: 788 calories, 29 grams protein, 53 grams carbohydrates, 54 grams total fat, 79 milligrams cholesterol, 764 milligrams sodium.

Cappelletti Pesto Salad

This version of cold pasta with pesto uses cappelletti, which resemble little hats, or another fancy-shaped pasta. Serve the salad with warm garlic bread and Italian-style cold cuts.

The basic pesto recipe makes enough for another meal—mix the pesto into hot tagliarini or spoon it over sliced sun-ripened tomatoes.

Pesto (recipe follows)
8 ounces cappelletti or other medium-size fancy-shaped dry pasta
⅓ cup olive oil
2 tablespoons white wine vinegar
1 clove garlic, minced or pressed
Freshly ground pepper (optional)

Prepare Pesto; set aside.

In a 5- to 6-quart pan, bring 3 quarts water to a boil over high heat. Add pasta; let water return to a boil and cook, uncovered, just until tender to bite (about 10 minutes). Or cook according to package directions. Drain, rinse with cold water, and drain well again.

In a large bowl, combine oil, vinegar, garlic, and ⅓ cup of the pesto; mix until well blended. Add pasta and mix gently. Cover and refrigerate for at least 1 hour or until next day. Just before serving, sprinkle with coarsely ground pepper, if desired. Makes 4 to 6 servings.

Pesto. In a blender or food processor, combine 1 cup lightly packed **fresh basil leaves,** ½ cup (2½ oz.) grated **Parmesan cheese,** and ¼ cup **olive oil;** add 1 clove minced **garlic,** if desired. Whirl until basil is finely chopped. Use at once; or place in a small jar, top with a thin layer of olive oil to keep pesto from darkening; and refrigerate for up to a week. Freeze for longer storage. Makes about ⅔ cup.

Per serving: 477 calories, 11 grams protein, 45 grams carbohydrates, 28 grams total fat, 7 milligrams cholesterol, 169 milligrams sodium.

Tortellini Salad

Cheese- or meat-filled tortellini and a variety of colorful vegetables vie for your attention in a hearty entrée salad.

4 cups broccoli flowerets
1 jar (6 oz.) marinated artichoke hearts
Tangy Dressing (recipe follows)
4 cups cooked cold tortellini or small ravioli
1½ cups *each* sliced mushrooms and halved cherry tomatoes
1 can (6 oz.) medium-size pitted ripe olives, drained
Salt

In a 4- to 5-quart pan, bring 2 quarts water to a boil over high heat. Add broccoli and cook, uncovered, just until tender-crisp when pierced (about 1 minute). Drain broccoli, rinse with cold water, and drain well.

Drain artichokes, reserving marinade. Prepare Tangy Dressing. In a large bowl, combine artichokes, tortellini, mushrooms, tomatoes, and olives; add dressing and mix until well coated. (At this point, you may cover and refrigerate tortellini mixture and broccoli separately until next day.)

Just before serving, add broccoli to tortellini mixture and mix lightly. Season with salt to taste. Makes 4 to 6 servings.

Tangy Dressing. Measure **reserved artichoke marinade** and add enough **salad oil** to make ⅓ cup. Stir in ⅓ cup **red wine vinegar,** 1 tablespoon *each* **dry basil** and **Dijon mustard,** 2 teaspoons **lemon juice,** and ½ teaspoon **pepper.**

Per serving (with cheese-filled tortellini): 370 calories, 14 grams protein, 30 grams carbohydrates, 23 grams total fat, 27 milligrams cholesterol, 681 milligrams sodium.

Cappelletti Pesto Salad

As a spunky alternative to macaroni salad, serve basil-dressed, hat-shaped cappelletti with cold sliced deli meats.

Lemon-Shrimp Pasta Salad

Soy, sesame oil, and ginger lend an Oriental emphasis to a lively main-dish salad of fettucine and shrimp.

  12 ounces dry fettuccine
   1 tablespoon sesame oil
  ⅓ cup chopped green onions
   1 tablespoon grated lemon peel

In a 3- to 4-quart pan, combine vinegar, lemon juice, honey, ginger, garlic, soy sauce, and red pepper; add shrimp. Bring to a boil over high heat, stirring occasionally; cover and immediately remove from heat. Let stand, stirring occasionally, until shrimp are opaque in center when slashed (about 10 minutes). Lift out shrimp with a slotted spoon, reserving cooking liquid. Cover and refrigerate shrimp.

Meanwhile, in a 5- to 6-quart pan, bring 3 quarts water to a boil over high heat. Add pasta; let water return to a boil and cook, uncovered, just until tender to bite (about 15 minutes). Or cook according to package directions. Drain, rinse with cold water, and drain well again.

In a large bowl, combine pasta, reserved cooking liquid, shrimp, sesame oil, onions, and lemon peel. Mix lightly, using 2 spoons, until well coated. If made ahead, cover and refrigerate until next day. Makes 4 to 6 servings.

Per serving: 350 calories, 27 grams protein, 49 grams carbohydrates, 4 grams total fat, 132 milligrams cholesterol, 421 milligrams sodium.

Lemon-Shrimp Pasta Salad

Fettuccine and cold shrimp mingle in a tantalizing dressing of honey, soy, and sesame oil. Complete the meal with fruit, sesame bread sticks, and sparkling mineral water.

  ¼ cup white wine vinegar
  3 tablespoons lemon juice
1½ tablespoons *each* honey and chopped fresh ginger
  1 clove garlic, minced or pressed
  1 tablespoon soy sauce
     Dash of ground red pepper (cayenne)
1½ pounds large shrimp, shelled and deveined

Corkscrew Pasta with Chiles, Chicken & Cheese

This hearty pasta salad, inspired by south-of-the-border flavors, has chunks of chicken, crisp bites of jicama, and a creamy, spicy dressing.

  8 ounces corkscrew pasta *(cavatappi), penne,* or other medium-size fancy-shaped dry pasta
  2 tablespoons salad oil
  ½ cup mayonnaise
  1 small can (4 oz.) diced green chiles

Corkscrew Pasta with Chiles, Chicken & Cheese

Twirled pasta combines cheerfully with chiles and jicama in this Mexican-accented summertime entrée.

1 large jar (4 oz.) diced pimentos, drained
1 teaspoon *each* oregano leaves and cumin seeds
2 teaspoons chili powder
1 tablespoon white wine vinegar
½ cup chopped green onions
1 cup finely diced jicama or celery
1½ cups diced or shredded cooked chicken, turkey, or ham
2 cups (8 oz.) shredded Cheddar cheese
1 can (about 2 oz.) sliced ripe olives, drained
Green leaf lettuce, washed and crisped
Fresh cilantro (coriander) or parsley sprigs

In a 5- to 6-quart pan, bring 3 quarts water to a boil over high heat. Add pasta; let water return to a boil and cook, uncovered, just until tender to bite (12 to 14 minutes). Or cook according to package directions. Drain, rinse with cold water, and drain well again.

Meanwhile, in a large bowl, combine oil, mayonnaise, green chiles, pimentos, oregano, cumin seeds, chili powder, and vinegar; mix until well blended.

Add pasta, onions, jicama, chicken, cheese, and half the olives to dressing. Mix lightly until well coated.

Line a salad bowl or serving platter with lettuce; mound salad on lettuce. Garnish with remaining olives and cilantro. Makes 6 servings.

Per serving: 567 calories, 25 grams protein, 34 grams carbohydrates, 37 grams total fat, 82 milligrams cholesterol, 588 milligrams sodium.

Pasta & Pepper Salad

Tiny, rice-shaped pasta, known as orzo, and colorful flecks of red or green bell pepper come together in this cold pasta salad. Serve it as a side dish in a cold buffet of sliced meats and crisp vegetables.

4 ounces orzo
¼ cup olive oil or salad oil
2½ tablespoons white wine vinegar
1½ teaspoons dry basil
1 small clove garlic, minced or pressed
3 tablespoons grated Parmesan cheese
½ teaspoon salt
⅛ teaspoon pepper
1 tablespoon chopped parsley
½ cup finely chopped red or green bell pepper

In a 4- to 5-quart pan, bring about 2 quarts water to a boil over high heat. Add pasta; let water return to a boil and cook, uncovered, just until tender to bite (about 25 minutes). Or cook according to package directions. Drain, rinse with cold water, and drain well again.

In a large bowl, combine oil, vinegar, basil, garlic, cheese, salt, and pepper; mix until well blended. Add pasta and stir until well coated. Cover and refrigerate for at least 4 hours or until next day. Just before serving, stir in parsley and bell pepper. Makes 6 servings.

Per serving: 165 calories, 4 grams protein, 15 grams carbohydrates, 10 grams total fat, 2 milligrams cholesterol, 231 milligrams sodium.

Caper Egg Salad in Pasta Shells

Giant macaroni shells filled with caper-studded egg salad make a stylish warm-weather luncheon dish. A chilled blush wine, such as white zinfandel, is a refreshing complement.

2 tablespoons salad oil
16 or 20 giant pasta shells
    Caper Egg Salad (recipe follows)
    Green leaf lettuce, washed and crisped (optional)
    Celery leaves (optional)

Fill a large bowl with about 2 quarts cold water; add oil and set aside.

In a 5- to 6-quart pan, bring about 3 quarts water to a boil over high heat. Add pasta; let water return to a boil and cook, uncovered, until barely tender to bite (about 10 minutes). Or cook according to package directions. Remove pasta shells individually to avoid tearing. Immerse in the cold water until completely cooled; drain well again. Pat dry with paper towels.

Prepare Caper Egg Salad. Fill each shell with salad. Arrange 1 or 2 lettuce leaves, if desired, on individual dinner plates. Set 4 or 5 shells on each plate and garnish with celery leaves, if desired. If made ahead, cover and refrigerate for up to 4 hours. Makes 4 servings.

Caper Egg Salad. Combine ⅓ cup **sour cream,** 2 tablespoons *each* **Dijon mustard** and drained **capers,** ¾ cup thinly sliced **celery,** and 3 tablespoons thinly sliced **green onions;** mix until well blended. Peel and chop 6 hard-cooked **eggs;** add to sour cream mixture and mix lightly until well blended. Season with **salt** and **pepper** to taste.

Per serving: 436 calories, 17 grams protein, 45 grams carbohydrates, 20 grams total fat, 419 milligrams cholesterol, 467 milligrams sodium.

Lasagne Wheels with Radish Salad

Frilly edged lasagne noodles are filled with a radish and prosciutto salad. Serve these pinwheels as an unusual summer entrée.

2 tablespoons salad oil
12 lasagne noodles, *each* about 1½ inches wide and 10 inches long
    Radish Salad (recipe follows)
    Watercress sprigs, washed and crisped
4 to 6 radishes

Fill a large bowl with about 2 quarts cold water; add oil and set aside.

In a 5- to 6-quart pan, bring about 3 quarts water to a boil over high heat. Add pasta; let water return to a boil and cook, uncovered, just until tender to bite (about 10 minutes). Or cook according to package directions. Drain pasta carefully to avoid tearing. Immerse in the cold water until completely cooled; drain well again. Pat dry with paper towels.

Prepare Radish Salad. Lay lasagne flat; spread about ¼ cup of the salad on each noodle. Starting at a narrow end, roll each into a pinwheel.

Arrange 6 to 8 watercress sprigs on individual dinner plates. Set 2 or 3 pinwheels, edges up, on each plate and garnish with a radish. If made ahead, cover and refrigerate for up to 4 hours. Makes 4 to 6 servings.

Radish Salad. Combine 11 to 12 ounces **cream cheese,** softened; 2 tablespoons **white wine vinegar;** and 1½ teaspoons minced **fresh tarragon** or ½ teaspoon dry tarragon. Mix until smooth and creamy. Lightly stir in 6 ounces thinly sliced **prosciutto** or pastrami, cut into thin slivers; 1¼ cups lightly packed shredded **watercress sprigs;** ¾ cup chopped **radishes;** and ⅓ cup thinly sliced **chives.** Season with **salt** and **pepper** to taste.

Per serving: 458 calories, 16 grams protein, 42 grams carbohydrates, 26 grams total fat, 73 milligrams cholesterol, 559 milligrams sodium.

Caper Egg Salad in Pasta Shells

Oversize pasta shells brim with a flavorful cargo of creamy, caper-flecked egg salad. As a jaunty garnish, add a sprig of celery leaves.

Tabbuli

Colorfully garnished with tomatoes and mint and wreathed with small romaine leaves, this Middle Eastern cracked wheat salad is a party favorite. You can make it several days ahead.

- 1 cup *each* bulgur wheat and cold water
- ½ cup *each* minced parsley and green onions
- ¼ cup chopped green bell pepper
- ¼ cup fresh mint leaves or 2 tablespoons dry mint
- 1 large tomato, peeled and chopped
- ¼ cup *each* olive oil and lemon juice
  Salt
  Small romaine lettuce leaves, washed and crisped
  Tomato wedges

Rinse bulgur several times; combine with cold water and let stand for 1 hour. Drain any liquid that is not absorbed.

In a large bowl, mix bulgur with parsley, onions, bell pepper, mint, chopped tomato, olive oil, and lemon juice. Season with salt to taste. Cover and refrigerate for at least 1 hour or up to 3 days.

Mound tabbuli in a serving bowl and surround with lettuce and tomatoes. To eat, scoop tabbuli onto lettuce leaves; top servings with tomato wedges. Makes 6 to 8 servings.

Per serving: 147 calories, 2 grams protein, 20 grams carbohydrates, 7 grams total fat, 0 milligram cholesterol, 22 milligrams sodium.

Crunchy Rice, Bean & Ham Salad

Whether you use a small amount of ham and offer it as a side dish, or include lots of ham and serve it as a main course, this zesty salad is sure to please.

- 3 cups cooked rice
- 1 can (about 15 oz.) kidney beans, drained
- 1½ cups sliced celery
- ½ cup *each* chopped green onions and green bell pepper
- 1 jar (2 oz.) sliced pimentos, drained
- 4 to 8 ounces cooked ham, cut into thin strips
  Sweet-Sour Dressing (recipe follows)
  Lettuce leaves, washed and crisped
- 1 or 2 tomatoes, cut into wedges
- 1 or 2 hard-cooked eggs, sliced

In a large bowl, combine rice, beans, celery, onions, bell pepper, pimentos, and ham. Prepare Sweet-Sour Dressing and pour over rice mixture; mix gently, lifting with 2 forks, until well coated. Cover and refrigerate, stirring occasionally, for at least 8 hours or until next day.

Line a salad bowl or serving platter with lettuce. Mound salad on lettuce and garnish with tomatoes and eggs. Makes 6 to 8 servings.

Sweet-Sour Dressing. In a small pan, combine ⅓ cup **cider vinegar**, 3 tablespoons **sugar**, ¼ cup **salad oil**, 2 tablespoons **Dijon mustard**, 2 teaspoons **garlic salt**, 1 teaspoon **pepper**, and ¼ teaspoon **liquid hot pepper seasoning**. Heat, stirring, until mixture is well blended and comes to a boil.

Per serving: 302 calories, 13 grams protein, 37 grams carbohydrates, 11 grams total fat, 85 milligrams cholesterol, 1,219 milligrams sodium.

Molded Mexican Rice Salad

Cherry tomatoes brighten this rice salad ring seasoned with a piquant chili-flavored dressing. It's a good side dish with barbecued chicken.

- 2 cups long-grain white rice
  Creamy Chili Dressing (recipe follows)
- 1 small green bell pepper, seeded and chopped
- ½ cup chopped green onions
- 1 small can (2¼ oz.) sliced ripe olives, drained
  About 1 tablespoon mayonnaise
- 2 cups halved cherry tomatoes
  Lettuce leaves, washed and crisped (optional)
  Fresh cilantro (coriander) sprigs (optional)

Cook rice according to package directions until tender to bite. Transfer to a large bowl and let cool slightly.

Sushi Salad

Capture the elusive Eastern essence of sushi with only half the effort in this beautifully composed rice salad.

Prepare Creamy Chili Dressing; add to rice along with bell pepper, onions, and olives. Mix lightly until well coated. Grease a 2-quart ring mold with mayonnaise. Firmly press rice mixture into mold, cover, and refrigerate for at least 6 hours or until next day.

To unmold salad, run a knife around edge of mold. Place a serving platter over mold; invert both and shake firmly to transfer salad to platter. Fill center of salad with tomatoes. Garnish with lettuce and cilantro, if desired. Makes 6 servings.

Creamy Chili Dressing. Mix ¾ cup **mayonnaise,** 5 tablespoons **white wine vinegar,** 2½ teaspoons **chili powder,** ¼ teaspoon ground **cumin,** and 1 small can (4 oz.) diced **green chiles.**

Per serving: 490 calories, 6 grams protein, 58 grams carbohydrates, 26 grams total fat, 18 milligrams cholesterol, 384 milligrams sodium.

Sushi Salad

This sushi-style rice salad is garnished with butter-flied shrimp and delicately seasoned vegetables. Serve with jasmine tea for a refreshing meal.

- 1 **large carrot**
- ⅓ **cup seasoned rice vinegar (or ⅓ cup rice or distilled white vinegar mixed with 3 tablespoons sugar and salt to taste)**
- ¼ **teaspoon chili oil**
- 2 **teaspoons sesame oil**
- ⅔ **cup frozen tiny peas, thawed**
- 1 **pound medium-size butterflied cooked shrimp**
  Sushi Rice (recipe follows)
  Spinach leaves
  Pickled red ginger strips (optional)

Cut carrot into 3-inch-long matchstick pieces. In a 2- to 3-quart pan, bring vinegar to a boil. Add carrots; cook, stirring often, just until tender-crisp to bite (about 30 seconds). Drain; reserve and refrigerate cooking liquid. Stir chili oil into carrots; set aside. Stir sesame oil into peas; set aside.

In a medium-size bowl, combine chilled cooking liquid and shrimp; let stand for about 10 minutes. Drain and discard liquid. (At this point, you may cover and refrigerate carrots, peas, and shrimp separately until next day.)

Prepare Sushi Rice. Line individual salad plates with spinach. Mound rice on top; surround with carrots, peas, and shrimp. Garnish with red ginger, if desired. Makes 4 to 6 servings.

Sushi Rice. In a 1½- to 2-quart pan, rinse 1½ cups **short-grain (pearl) rice** with water until water is clear; drain. Add 1¾ cups water to rice. Cover and bring to a boil over high heat. Reduce heat and simmer until water is absorbed (about 15 minutes). Stir in ¼ cup **seasoned rice vinegar** (or substitute ¼ cup rice or distilled white vinegar mixed with 2 tablespoons sugar and salt to taste). Let rice cool. If made ahead, cover and let stand at room temperature until next day.

Per serving: 348 calories, 23 grams protein, 56 grams carbohydrates, 3 grams total fat, 114 milligrams cholesterol, 186 milligrams sodium.

WHOLE-GRAIN SALADS

As grains in less familiar forms become more available, it isn't long before they turn up in a salad bowl. These recipes feature couscous and wheat berries.

Brown Berry & Mushroom Salad

Cooked wheat berries are intriguingly chewy and have a sweet, nutlike flavor. Here, they combine with fresh vegetables in a nourishing salad.

- 1 cup **wheat berries**
- 3 cups **water**
  Oregano Dressing (recipe follows)
- ¼ pound **mushrooms,** thinly sliced
- 1 cup **pitted ripe olives**
- ¼ cup chopped **green onions**
- 1 **green bell pepper,** seeded and sliced into rings

In a 3- to 4-quart pan, combine wheat berries and water. Bring to a boil over high heat; reduce heat, cover, and simmer until grain is tender to bite (about 2 hours). Rinse and drain. (At this point, you may cover and refrigerate for up to a week.)

Prepare Oregano Dressing. In a salad bowl, combine cooked wheat berries, dressing, mushrooms, and olives. Cover and refrigerate for at least 1 hour.

Just before serving, stir in onions. Garnish salad with bell pepper rings. Makes 6 servings.

Curried Couscous Salad

Middle Eastern and Indian cuisines unite in this couscous salad dressed with curried yogurt and served with lamb kebabs.

Oregano Dressing. Mix ¼ cup *each* **salad oil** and **white wine vinegar;** 1 clove **garlic,** minced or pressed; 1 tablespoon **Dijon mustard;** 1½ teaspoons **oregano leaves;** ¼ teaspoon **salt;** and ⅛ teaspoon **pepper.**

Per serving: 234 calories, 5 grams protein, 23 grams carbohydrates, 15 grams total fat, 0 milligram cholesterol, 339 milligrams sodium.

Curried Couscous Salad

Couscous is made from semolina, one of the products of milling hard or durum wheat. Though hard when purchased, couscous quickly becomes soft and fluffy when added to boiling water. It's delicious in a salad with almonds and dried apricots.

- 2 cups **water**
- 2 **chicken bouillon cubes**
- 1 cup **couscous**
- ⅓ cup **slivered almonds**
  Curry Dressing (recipe follows)
- 2 small **zucchini** (about ¾ lb. *total*), thinly sliced
- ½ cup *each* **raisins** and coarsely chopped **dried apricots**
  Romaine lettuce leaves
  Dried apricot halves
  Mint sprigs

In a 2- to 3-quart pan, bring water and bouillon cubes to a boil over high heat, stirring until bouillon cubes are dissolved. Add couscous and stir until well moistened. Remove from heat, cover, and let stand until liquid is absorbed and couscous is tender (about 20 minutes).

Spread almonds in a shallow baking pan; toast in a 350° oven until golden (about 8 minutes).

Prepare Curry Dressing. Stir cooked couscous well with a fork to separate grains. Add dressing, zucchini, raisins, chopped apricots, and almonds; cover and refrigerate for at least 2 hours or until next day.

Just before serving, line a platter with lettuce leaves and mound salad in center. Garnish with apricot halves and mint. Makes 8 to 10 servings.

Curry Dressing. Combine 1½ cups **plain yogurt;** 2 tablespoons *each* **lemon juice** and **Major Grey's chutney,** chopped; 2 teaspoons **curry powder;** and ¼ teaspoon *each* **dry mustard, ground ginger,** and **ground cinnamon.** Season with **ground red pepper** (cayenne) to taste. Stir until well blended.

Per serving: 172 calories, 6 grams protein, 28 grams carbohydrates, 3 grams total fat, 2 milligrams cholesterol, 226 milligrams sodium.

Fresh Fruit Salads

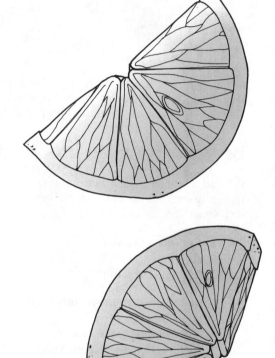

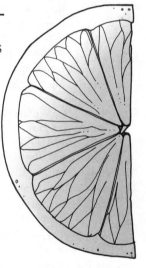

Naturally elegant, fresh fruits are also natural choices for salads. Let their rich, appetizing colors and flavors come forward with as little embellishment as possible, and keep dressings light.

Citrus fruits, especially, mix effectively with mild greens and sweet onions in a delicious counterpoint of contrasting flavors. Try the Orange & Onion Salad—a good meal opener that also enhances roasted meats, smoked ham, or turkey.

Sweeter fruit creations, such as Kiwi Fruit Salad, can be served as a luncheon entrée or even as a dessert. ▨

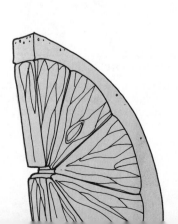

Orange & Onion Salad

Orange slices and sweet red onions are a classic salad combination. Here, a creamy avocado dressing and sliced cucumber add a new dimension.

> **Avocado Dressing (recipe follows)**
> 2 **large or 3 small oranges**
> 2 **thin slices red onion**
> 1 **cup firmly packed alfalfa sprouts**
> 1 **cup thin cucumber slices**

Prepare Avocado Dressing; set aside.

Cut off peel and white membrane from oranges. Cut oranges crosswise into ¼-inch-thick slices. Cut onion slices in half crosswise; separate into strips.

Spread alfalfa sprouts on individual salad plates. Overlap orange and cucumber slices on top of sprouts. Spoon dressing over each salad and garnish with onion. Makes 4 servings.

Avocado Dressing. Pit and peel 1 small ripe **avocado.** Place in a blender or food processor; add ⅛ teaspoon **ground red pepper** (cayenne) and ¼ cup *each* **sour cream** and **lemon juice.** Whirl until smooth. If made ahead, cover and refrigerate until next day.

Per serving: 156 calories, 3 grams protein, 17 grams carbohydrates, 10 grams total fat, 6 milligrams cholesterol, 16 milligrams sodium.

Avocado & Oranges with Jalapeño Dressing

Yogurt tames the heat of fresh jalapeño chile in this nippy dressing just as the mellow avocado balances the tart, juicy oranges.

> **Jalapeño Dressing (recipe follows)**
> 3 **large oranges**
> 2 **large ripe avocados**
> **Large iceberg lettuce leaves, washed and crisped**
> ½ **small cucumber, thinly sliced**
> **Fresh cilantro (coriander) sprigs**
> 1 **fresh jalapeño chile, cut into thin crosswise slices (optional)**

Prepare Jalapeño Dressing; set aside.

Cut off peel and white membrane from oranges. Cut crosswise into thin slices. Cut avocados in half lengthwise; pit and peel.

Place lettuce leaves on individual salad plates. Arrange orange and cucumber slices and an avocado half on each plate; spoon dressing over each salad. Garnish with cilantro sprigs and, if desired, jalapeño slices. Makes 4 servings.

Jalapeño Dressing. Combine ½ cup **plain yogurt;** ¼ teaspoon crushed **cumin seeds;** 1 clove **garlic,** minced or pressed; 2 to 3 tablespoons stemmed, seeded, and minced **fresh or canned jalapeño chile;** and 2 tablespoons chopped fresh **cilantro** (coriander). Mix until well blended. Season with **salt** to taste. If made ahead, cover and refrigerate until next day.

Per serving: 341 calories, 6 grams protein, 31 grams carbohydrates, 25 grams total fat, 2 milligrams cholesterol, 130 milligrams sodium.

Chicken-stuffed Melon with Pomegranate

For a visual treat, fill cantaloupe halves with chicken salad; top with green grapes and crimson pomegranate seeds. To remove the seeds from a pomegranate, follow the directions in Mixed Winter Fruit Salad, page 70. *(Pictured on page 95.)*

> 2 **medium-size cantaloupe melons**
> 2 **cups diced cold cooked chicken**
> ½ **cup seedless green grapes**
> **Seeds from 1 medium-size pomegranate**
> 1 **small kiwi fruit, peeled and sliced**
> **Lime-Honey Dressing (recipe follows)**

Cut each cantaloupe in half in a zigzag pattern. Scoop out and discard seeds. With a curved grapefruit knife, cut fruit from rind, then into bite-size pieces. Drain melon pieces and shells.

Combine melon and chicken; spoon into shells. Top with grapes, pomegranate seeds, and kiwi slices. Prepare Lime-Honey Dressing; pass dressing at the table. Makes 4 servings.

Per serving: 276 calories, 23 grams protein, 35 grams carbohydrates, 6 grams total fat, 62 milligrams cholesterol, 86 milligrams sodium.

Lime-Honey Dressing. Mix 4 tablespoons *each* **lime juice** and **honey** with ¼ teaspoon *each* **ground coriander** and **nutmeg.**

Per tablespoon: 34 calories, .04 gram protein, 9 grams carbohydrates, .03 gram total fat, 0 milligram cholesterol, 2 milligrams sodium.

Mixed Winter Fruit Salad

Combine such distinctive early winter fruits as persimmons, tangerines, grapefruit, and pomegranate seeds with equally stylish greens—Belgian endive and watercress—for a spectacular salad.

6 large firm-ripe, crisp persimmons, such as Fuyu

6 large tight-skinned tangerines or mandarins, such as Clementine or Murcott Honey

3 large pink grapefruit

1 medium-size pomegranate

1 medium-size head Belgian endive, washed and crisped

2 cups lightly packed watercress sprigs, washed and crisped

Honey-Mustard Dressing (recipe follows)

Salt and pepper

With a sharp paring knife, peel persimmons. Holding fruit over a bowl, cut into wedges and place in bowl.

Cut off peel and white membrane from tangerines and grapefruit. Holding fruit over bowl with persimmons, cut between inner membranes; remove segments and add to persimmons. Set aside.

To seed pomegranate, cut off crown end. Score peel lengthwise to divide fruit into quarters. To prevent staining your hands and clothes, immerse fruit in a bowl of water; break pomegranate apart along scored lines and with your fingers loosen seeds from pulp and skin. Remove pulp and skin from water and discard. Drain seeds and set aside.

With a slotted spoon, lift out persimmons, tangerines, and grapefruit from their juices and transfer to a large salad bowl (reserve juice for other uses, if desired). Add pomegranate seeds, endive leaves, and watercress sprigs to salad. Prepare Honey-Mustard Dressing; pour over salad and mix lightly until well coated. Pass salt and pepper at the table. Makes 12 servings.

Honey-Mustard Dressing. Combine ¼ cup **salad oil,** 3 tablespoons **cider vinegar,** 1½ tablespoons **Dijon mustard,** 2 teaspoons **honey,** and ¼ teaspoon **dry tarragon.** Mix until well blended.

Per serving: 232 calories, 2 grams protein, 50 grams carbohydrates, 5 grams total fat, 0 milligram cholesterol, 60 milligrams sodium.

Spinach & Fruit Salad

Choose from such dramatic-looking and exotically flavored fruits as carambola (star fruit), kiwi fruit, mango, and papaya to make this stunning salad. Feature one fruit or an assortment. The dressing is made with aromatic passion fruit.

Passion Fruit Dressing (recipe follows)

1 pound spinach, washed and crisped

1 small red onion, thinly sliced and separated into rings

2 cups sliced ripe carambola (unpeeled), kiwi fruit (peeled), mango (pitted and peeled), or papaya (seeded and peeled), or a combination

Prepare Passion Fruit Dressing; set aside.

Remove and discard coarse spinach stems. Arrange spinach leaves in concentric circles on individual salad plates. Decoratively arrange onion rings and fruit slices on spinach. If made ahead, cover and refrigerate for up to 1 hour. Pass dressing at the table. Makes 4 servings.

Per serving: 65 calories, 3 grams protein, 15 grams carbohydrates, .52 gram total fat, 0 milligram cholesterol, 67 milligrams sodium.

Passion Fruit Dressing. Cut 2 or 3 **passion fruit** in half; spoon out seeds and pulp to measure ¼ cup. Place in a blender or food processor and whirl until seeds resemble ground pepper. Add 6 tablespoons **lemon juice,** 2 tablespoons **sugar,** and 1 teaspoon *each* grated **lemon peel** and **dry mustard;** whirl until combined. With motor running, pour in ¾ cup **salad oil** and whirl until well blended. Season with **salt** to taste. If made ahead, cover and refrigerate for up to 3 days. Makes about 1¼ cups.

Per tablespoon: 81 calories, .08 gram protein, 2 grams carbohydrates, 8 grams total fat, 0 milligram cholesterol, 2 milligrams sodium.

Mixed Winter Fruit Salad

Brighten up early winter menus with vivid citrus, persimmons, and pomegranate seeds in this dramatic seasonal salad.

Lady Apples with Cheese & Greens

Halved lady apples, as delicious as they are decorative, mingle with blue cheese in an appetizing starter salad.

Prepare Blue Cheese Dressing; drizzle lettuce with some of the dressing. Nestle 6 apple halves, 1 or 2 pieces of cheese, and 3 almonds alongside lettuce on each plate. Scatter pomegranate seeds over apples. Pass remaining dressing and salt and pepper at the table. Makes 4 servings.

Per serving: 541 calories, 15 grams protein, 70 grams carbohydrates, 26 grams total fat, 44 milligrams cholesterol, 853 milligrams sodium.

Blue Cheese Dressing. Combine ⅓ cup **salad oil,** 3 tablespoons **white wine vinegar,** and 1 tablespoon *each* **Dijon mustard** and minced **shallot** or onion. Mix until well blended. Stir in 2 tablespoons crumbled **blue-veined cheese.**

Per tablespoon: 56 calories, .28 gram protein, .44 gram carbohydrates, 6 grams total fat, .97 milligram cholesterol, 53 milligrams sodium.

Lady Apples with Cheese & Greens

Diminutive lady apples, a choice autumn fruit, are complemented by blue cheese and pomegranate seeds in this colorful first-course salad. To remove pomegranate seeds, follow directions in Mixed Winter Fruit Salad, page 70.

12	**lady apples** (*each* about 1½ inches in diameter)
	Lemon juice
¼ to ½	**pound blue-veined cheese**
1½	**quarts lightly packed red leaf lettuce,** washed and crisped
	Blue Cheese Dressing (recipe follows)
12	**unblanched almonds**
¼	**cup pomegranate seeds**
	Salt and pepper

Cut lady apples in half lengthwise and remove stems and cores. Moisten cut surfaces with lemon juice. Cut cheese into 4 or 8 pieces. Tear lettuce into bite-size pieces; arrange on individual salad plates.

Chutney, Cheese & Fruit Salad

Light and colorful, this salad combines fresh summer fruits and dilled cottage cheese. The dressing is also good with chicken salad or a curried rice salad.

	Chutney Dressing (recipe follows)
2	**cups cottage cheese**
2	**tablespoons chopped fresh dill or** 2 to 3 teaspoons dill weed
16	**medium-size strawberries or** 1 large peach or nectarine
2	**medium-size ripe bananas**
2	**large kiwi fruit**
4	**large green leaf lettuce leaves,** washed and crisped
1	**cup seedless grapes or 24 sweet cherries**

Kiwi Fruit Salad

A few kiwi fruit add a colorful and flavorful dimension to an autumn fruit salad, drizzled with honey-yogurt dressing and garnished with nuts.

Prepare Chutney Dressing; set aside 1 cup (reserve remaining dressing for other uses).

In a medium-size bowl, mix cottage cheese and dill; set aside.

Hull strawberries (or peel peach, if desired; pit and cut into 16 wedges). Cut bananas into ¼-inch-thick slices. Peel kiwi fruit and cut into ¼-inch-thick slices.

Arrange lettuce on individual dinner plates. Mound ½ cup of the cheese mixture onto center of each leaf and surround with strawberries, banana and kiwi slices, and grapes. Spoon about 1 tablespoon of the dressing over each portion of cheese. Pour remaining ¾ cup dressing into a serving bowl and pass at the table. Makes 4 servings.

Per serving: 298 calories, 15 grams protein, 35 grams carbohydrates, 12 grams total fat, 16 milligrams cholesterol, 448 milligrams sodium.

Chutney Dressing. In a blender or food processor, combine 3 large cloves **garlic**, 1 tablespoon chopped **fresh ginger**, 1½ tablespoons prepared **coarse-grained mustard**, ½ cup **Major Grey's chutney**, and ⅓ cup **raspberry wine vinegar** or red wine vinegar; whirl until puréed.

With motor running, slowly pour in 1 cup **salad oil**; whirl until dressing is thick. If made ahead, cover and refrigerate for up to 1 month. Makes 2 cups.

Per tablespoon: 72 calories, .10 gram protein, 3 grams carbohydrates, 7 grams total fat, 0 milligram cholesterol, 16 milligrams sodium.

Kiwi Fruit Salad

Translucent green slices of kiwi fruit accent this glittering mélange of pineapple, banana, persimmons, and grapes.

Honey-Yogurt Dressing (recipe follows)
1 **medium-size pineapple, peeled, cored, and cut into 1-inch cubes**
3 **ripe bananas, sliced diagonally**
2 **firm-ripe, crisp persimmons, such as Fuyu, thinly sliced**
1 **cup red grapes (about ½ lb.)**
6 **kiwi fruit, peeled and sliced crosswise**
About 1 cup chopped pecans or walnuts

Prepare Honey-Yogurt Dressing; set aside.

In a large salad bowl, combine pineapple, bananas, persimmons, grapes, and kiwi fruit; mix gently. Cover and refrigerate for 30 minutes. Place nuts and dressing in individual bowls and pass at the table. Makes 6 servings.

Per serving: 309 calories, 3 grams protein, 48 grams carbohydrates, 15 grams total fat, 0 milligram cholesterol, 6 milligrams sodium.

Honey-Yogurt Dressing. Combine 1½ tablespoons grated **orange peel**, 1 teaspoon grated **fresh ginger**, ¾ cup *each* **mayonnaise** and **plain yogurt**, 2 tablespoons **honey**, and 1 tablespoon **lemon juice**. Mix until well blended. If made ahead, cover and refrigerate until next day.

Per tablespoon: 53 calories, .39 gram protein, 2 grams carbohydrates, 5 grams total fat, 4 milligram cholesterol, 39 milligrams sodium.

Melon, Cucumber & Tomato Salad

This summertime salad combines a tangy lemon-mint dressing with juicy casaba melon, tomatoes, and cucumber.

- ½ **cup salad oil**
- ¼ **cup lemon or lime juice**
- 2 **teaspoons sugar**
- ½ **teaspoon salt**
- ¼ **teaspoon pepper**
- 1 **tablespoon** *each* **finely chopped parsley and fresh mint leaves**
- 1 **casaba or small honeydew melon**
- 1 **small English cucumber, peeled (if desired) and thinly sliced**
- 4 **large firm-ripe tomatoes (about 2 lbs.), peeled and cubed**

Combine oil, lemon juice, sugar, salt, pepper, parsley, and mint. Mix until well blended. If made ahead, cover and refrigerate until next day.

About 1 hour before serving, cut melon in half; scoop out seeds. Cut melon into thin wedges and remove rind. In a salad bowl, combine melon, cucumber, and tomatoes. Stir dressing again; pour over salad and mix gently until well coated. Cover and let stand at room temperature for about 45 minutes, stirring once or twice. Makes 6 to 8 servings.

Per serving: 190 calories, 2 grams protein, 18 grams carbohydrates, 14 grams total fat, 0 milligram cholesterol, 159 milligrams sodium.

Three-color Fruit Salad

Avocados, papayas, and strawberries sparkle when topped with a light dressing made with the unfermented juice of wine grapes. Any juice remaining after you've prepared the dressing makes refreshing nonalcoholic sipping.

Three-color Fruit Salad

A dressing made from yogurt, candied ginger, and white wine grape juice splashes lightly over this eye-catching salad.

Wine Grape Dressing (recipe follows)
- 2 **medium-size ripe papayas**
- 3 **medium-size ripe avocados**
- 4 **to 5 cups strawberries**
- 2 **tablespoons toasted almonds (optional)**
  Watercress sprigs
  Salt

Prepare Wine Grape Dressing; set aside. Peel and seed papayas; slice into slender wedges. Pit and peel avocados; cut into thick slices. Hull strawberries and cut in half. Arrange portions of papaya, avocado, and strawberries on individual plates. Sprinkle with almonds, if desired, and garnish with watercress. Pass dressing and salt at the table. Makes 6 servings.

Per serving: 244 calories, 3 grams protein, 27 grams carbohydrates, 16 grams total fat, 0 milligram cholesterol, 15 milligrams sodium.

Wine Grape Dressing. Combine ¼ teaspoon **paprika** and 2 tablespoons *each* minced **crystallized ginger** and **plain yogurt;** mix until well blended. Whisking constantly, pour in ½ cup **white wine grape juice** (such as White Riesling, Gewürztraminer, French Colombard, Semillon, or white grape juice), 3 tablespoons **white wine vinegar,** and 1 tablespoon **salad oil.**

Per tablespoon: 27 calories, .13 gram protein, 4 grams carbohydrates, 1 gram total fat, .14 milligram cholesterol, 4 milligrams sodium.

PREVENTING CUT FRUITS FROM DARKENING

Once cut, some fruits—notably apples, apricots, avocados, bananas, peaches, and pears—begin to darken as cut surfaces are exposed to the air. To prevent this color change, brush cut surfaces with lemon or lime juice.

You can also use an ascorbic acid (vitamin C) powder intended for preserving the color of frozen fruits. Simply follow the package directions for serving fresh fruit.

Covered and refrigerated, cut fruits treated with lemon juice or ascorbic acid will be protected for up to 4 hours; or leave them at room temperature for up to 2 hours.

Molded Salads

Glistening settings for fruits and vegetables, molded salads are as convenient as they are attractive. You can prepare them well before the meal and then present them in all their shimmering beauty when it's time to eat.

Our salads take shape in a variety of traditional molds, ranging from facsimiles of fish to purely decorative rings. But you can form these salads in everyday containers as well, such as in the delicate teacups used in Rosy Apple Teacup Salads. ▪

Molded Chicken & Vegetable Salad

Made ahead and waiting in the refrigerator, this chicken salad loaf is a summertime treasure. Garnish it with garden-fresh slices of tomato and cucumber.

- ¼ cup cold water
- 1 envelope unflavored gelatin
- 1 chicken bouillon cube, crushed
- 1½ cups regular-strength chicken broth
- ¼ cup white wine vinegar
- ½ cup mayonnaise
- 1 teaspoon Dijon mustard
- 2 cups finely diced cooked chicken
- ¼ cup *each* thinly sliced green onions and sliced ripe olives
- ½ cup finely diced sweet pickles
- 1 cup thawed frozen peas
  Salt and pepper
  Sliced tomato
  Sliced cucumber

Pour cold water into a 1- to 1½-quart pan and sprinkle with gelatin; let stand for about 5 minutes to soften. Add bouillon cube and broth; place over low heat and stir until gelatin and bouillon cube are dissolved. Remove from heat and stir in vinegar.

Transfer gelatin mixture to a large bowl and refrigerate (or set bowl in a larger bowl filled with ice cubes and stir) until mixture reaches the consistency of unbeaten egg whites (30 to 45 minutes in refrigerator, 10 to 15 minutes over ice).

Add mayonnaise and mustard; stir until smooth. Mix in chicken, onions, olives, pickles, and peas. Season with salt and pepper to taste. Transfer to a lightly oiled 5- by 9-inch loaf pan. Cover and refrigerate until set (at least 4 hours) or until next day.

To serve, unmold onto a serving plate (see page 83). Garnish with tomato and cucumber slices. Cut mold into 1-inch-thick slices. Makes about 8 servings.

Per serving: 219 calories, 13 grams protein, 8 grams carbohydrates, 15 grams total fat, 39 milligrams cholesterol, 615 milligrams sodium.

Green & Gold Vegetable Mold

Add sparkle to your buffet table with this colorful salad composed of layers of crisp raw vegetables in an apple- and lemon-flavored gelatin.

- 3 cups apple juice
- 2 envelopes unflavored gelatin
- ½ cup lemon juice
- 1 cup diced celery
- 4 cups shredded carrots (about 5 large)
- ½ cup *each* chopped green onions and green bell pepper
- 3 cups finely shredded cabbage
  Lemon Mayonnaise (recipe follows)

Pour apple juice into a 2- to 2½-quart pan and sprinkle with gelatin; let stand for about 5 minutes to soften. Place over low heat and stir until gelatin is dissolved. Remove from heat and stir in lemon juice.

Set pan in a large bowl filled with ice cubes. Stir until mixture reaches the consistency of unbeaten egg whites (about 10 minutes).

Combine celery with ½ cup of the gelatin mixture; spoon into a lightly oiled 5- by 9-inch loaf pan. Then combine carrots with 1½ cups of the gelatin mixture; gently spoon half the carrot mixture over celery layer. Sprinkle with onions and bell pepper.

Combine remaining gelatin with cabbage; carefully spoon over onion layer. Top with remaining carrot mixture, pressing surface lightly until level. Cover and refrigerate until set (at least 8 hours) or for up to 2 days.

Prepare Lemon Mayonnaise.

To serve, unmold onto a serving plate (see page 83). Pass mayonnaise at the table. Makes 12 servings.

Per serving: 59 calories, 2 grams protein, 13 grams carbohydrates, .19 gram total fat, 0 milligram cholesterol, 30 milligrams sodium.

Lemon Mayonnaise. Combine 1 cup **mayonnaise,** 2 teaspoons **Dijon mustard,** ¼ cup **lemon juice,** and ¼ teaspoon **pepper;** mix until smoothly blended. If made ahead, cover and refrigerate for up to a week. Makes about 1¼ cups.

Per tablespoon: 80 calories, .13 gram protein, .56 gram carbohydrates, 9 grams total fat, 6 milligrams cholesterol, 78 milligrams sodium.

Potato Salad Squares

Here, a familiar favorite takes on an unusual form: this potato salad, made with gelatin, is molded in a square pan. Present servings on butter lettuce leaves.

> 2 **large potatoes, cooked and peeled**
> 3½ **tablespoons white wine vinegar**
> ⅓ **cup chopped sweet pickles**
> 1 **teaspoon salt**
> **Dash of pepper**
> ½ **teaspoon dill weed**
> ⅓ **cup *each* sliced green onions and chopped celery**
> 1½ **cups regular-strength chicken broth**
> 1 **envelope unflavored gelatin**
> ½ **cup mayonnaise**
> 1 **teaspoon Dijon mustard**
> ¼ **cup chopped parsley**
> **Butter lettuce leaves, washed and crisped**
> 1 **hard-cooked egg, sliced**
> **Paprika**

Cut potatoes into ½-inch cubes (you should have 2 cups *total*). In a large bowl, combine 2½ tablespoons of the vinegar, pickles, salt, pepper, dill, onions, and celery. Add potatoes and mix lightly until well coated; set aside.

Pour broth into a 1-quart pan and sprinkle with gelatin; let stand for about 5 minutes to soften. Place over low heat and stir until gelatin is dissolved. Remove from heat and stir in remaining 1 tablespoon vinegar.

Set pan in a large bowl filled with ice cubes. Stir until mixture reaches the consistency of unbeaten egg whites (about 5 minutes).

Add mayonnaise and mustard; beat with a rotary beater until foamy. Add to potato mixture along with parsley. Fold in gelatin mixture, coating vegetables thoroughly. Spoon into a lightly oiled 9-inch square pan. Cover and refrigerate until firm (at least 6 hours) or until next day.

Just before serving, arrange lettuce on individual plates. Cut mold into squares and arrange on lettuce. Garnish with egg and sprinkle with paprika. Makes 9 servings.

Per serving: 150 calories, 3 grams protein, 11 grams carbohydrates, 10 grams total fat, 38 milligrams cholesterol, 578 milligrams sodium.

Turkey Salad with Chutney Aspic

Accompany cool turkey salad and sliced fruits with a shimmering and spicy aspic, made bold with chutney and sprigs of cilantro.

> 2 **cups apple juice**
> 2 **envelopes unflavored gelatin**
> ⅓ **cup finely chopped Major Grey's chutney**
> 1 **green onion, chopped**
> **Gingered Turkey Salad (recipe follows)**
> 1 **medium-size ripe papaya**
> ½ **medium-size pineapple**
> **Fresh cilantro (coriander) sprigs**

Pour apple juice into a 1- to 1½-quart pan and sprinkle with gelatin; let stand for about 5 minutes to soften. Place over low heat and stir until gelatin is dissolved. Remove from heat and set pan in a large bowl filled with ice cubes. Stir until mixture reaches the consistency of unbeaten egg whites (about 5 minutes). Stir in chutney and onion. Spoon into 5 or 6 individual lightly oiled metal molds (about ½-cup size). Cover and refrigerate until set (at least 4 hours) or until next day.

Meanwhile, prepare Gingered Turkey Salad.

Just before serving, unmold aspics onto a large plate (see page 83) and return to refrigerator. Peel and seed papaya; slice crosswise. Cut off pineapple stem; halve fruit lengthwise and remove core. With a curved pineapple or grapefruit knife, cut fruit from rind. Slice pineapple into crescent-shaped slices.

On 5 or 6 dinner plates, alternate papaya and pineapple slices. Mound turkey salad beside fruit. Place an aspic on each plate; garnish with cilantro. Makes 5 or 6 servings.

Gingered Turkey Salad. Mix 5 cups diced **cooked turkey** or chicken, 6 tablespoons **salad oil,** ¼ cup **lime juice,** ¼ teaspoon minced **fresh ginger,** and 2 stalks **celery,** thinly sliced. Season to taste with **salt** and **pepper.** Cover and refrigerate for at least 2 hours or until next day.

Per serving: 448 calories, 37 grams protein, 31 grams carbohydrates, 19 grams total fat, 90 milligrams cholesterol, 158 milligrams sodium.

Turkey Salad with Chutney Aspic

Glistening chutney aspic complements both its companions—gingery turkey salad and sliced tropical fruit.

Creamy Cucumber Salad Mold

Sculpted for a summer's menu, this mold combines lime gelatin with cool sour cream, shredded cucumber, and dill.

dissolved. In a small bowl, combine sour cream, mustard, dill, and vinegar; stir until smooth. Add sour cream mixture and cucumbers to gelatin mixture and stir until well blended. Pour into a lightly oiled 1-quart mold or 8 individual ½-cup molds. Cover and refrigerate until set (at least 6 hours) or until next day.

To serve, unmold onto a serving plate or individual plates (see page 83). Garnish with lettuce and tomatoes. Makes 8 servings.

Per serving: 111 calories, 2 grams protein, 13 grams carbohydrates, 6 grams total fat, 13 milligrams cholesterol, 156 milligrams sodium.

Creamy Cucumber Salad Mold

Sour cream flavored with dill and tarragon vinegar combines with lime-flavored gelatin and shredded cucumber to produce a taste that's reminiscent of homemade bread-and-butter pickles.

- 2 **medium-size cucumbers**
- 1 **package (3 oz.) lime-flavored gelatin**
- 1 **teaspoon beef-flavored instant bouillon**
- 1 **cup boiling water**
- 1 **cup sour cream**
- ½ **teaspoon dry mustard**
- ⅛ **teaspoon dill weed**
- 3 **tablespoons tarragon vinegar**
  Small inner red lettuce leaves, washed and crisped
  Red and yellow cherry tomatoes

Cut cucumbers in half lengthwise; scoop out and discard seeds. Coarsely shred cucumbers; drain well.

Meanwhile, combine gelatin and bouillon in a large bowl; add water and stir until gelatin is

Apple Cider Mold

Celery, almonds, and chunks of apple provide the crunch in this tart cider salad. Top servings with a dollop of creamy chutney dressing.

- 3 **cups apple cider**
- 2 **envelopes unflavored gelatin**
- ¼ **cup sugar**
- 1 **can (6 oz.) frozen lemonade concentrate, thawed**
- 2 **large red-skinned apples**
- ¼ **cup chopped celery**
- ¼ **cup slivered almonds**
  Chutney Dressing (recipe follows)

Pour 1 cup of the cider into a 1½- to 2-quart pan; sprinkle with gelatin and let stand for about 5 minutes to soften. Add sugar; place over low heat and stir until gelatin and sugar are dissolved. Remove from heat and set aside.

Pour lemonade concentrate into a large bowl. Core and dice apples, and mix with lemonade. Then, with a slotted spoon, lift out apples and set aside. Add lemonade and remaining 2 cups cider to gelatin

Rosy Apple Teacup Salads

A wonderful teatime treat, poached apples in a shimmering cinnamon-spiced gelatin fill delicate teacups.

mixture; stir until blended. Set pan in a large bowl filled with ice cubes and stir until mixture reaches the consistency of unbeaten egg whites (about 10 minutes). Stir in apples and celery.

Sprinkle almonds in a 6-cup mold; spoon gelatin mixture over nuts. Cover and refrigerate until firm (at least 3 hours) or until next day.

Meanwhile, prepare Chutney Dressing.

To serve, unmold salad onto a serving plate (see page 83). Pass dressing at the table. Makes 8 servings.

Per serving: 178 calories, 3 grams protein, 39 grams carbohydrates, 2 grams total fat, 0 milligram cholesterol, 9 milligrams sodium.

Chutney Dressing. Combine ½ cup **sour cream;** ¼ cup **Major Grey's chutney,** finely chopped; and 1 teaspoon grated **orange peel.** Stir until well blended. Makes about ¾ cup.

Per tablespoon: 34 calories, .35 gram protein, 4 grams carbohydrates, 2 grams total fat, 4 milligrams cholesterol, 16 milligrams sodium.

Rosy Apple Teacup Salads

For dessert or a teatime treat, nestle small poached apples in your prettiest teacups and surround with a spicy gelatin. Choose Golden Delicious, Jonathan, or Newtown pippin apples.

> **8 small apples (about 2 inches in diameter)**
> **3 cups water**
> **1¼ cups sugar**
> **¼ cup hot red cinnamon candies**
> **1 can (8 oz.) crushed pineapple, drained**
> **3 tablespoons slivered almonds**
> **1 cup apple juice**
> **1 envelope unflavored gelatin**
> **2 tablespoons lemon juice**

Peel and core apples; pare, if necessary, to fit wide, deep teacups.

In a 5- to 6-quart pan, combine water, sugar, and cinnamon candies; bring to a boil over high heat. Reduce heat, stand apples in syrup, and simmer, turning often, just until apples are tender when pierced (about 10 minutes). Lift apples from syrup and transfer to teacups. Reserve 1 cup of the syrup.

In a small bowl, combine pineapple and almonds; spoon into apples, sprinkling any excess over tops. Set aside.

Pour apple juice into a 1- to 1½-quart pan and sprinkle with gelatin; let stand for about 5 minutes to soften. Place over low heat and stir until gelatin is dissolved. Remove from heat and stir in reserved 1 cup syrup and lemon juice. Pour gelatin mixture over apples. Cover and refrigerate until set (at least 4 hours) or until next day. Makes 8 servings.

Per serving: 250 calories, 2 grams protein, 59 grams carbohydrates, 2 grams total fat, 0 milligram cholesterol, 5 milligrams sodium.

Layered Fruit in Wine Mold

Glistening layers of strawberries, apricots, and grapes are set into a wine-flavored gelatin in this impressive-looking molded salad. Making it requires patience, but the finished product is so pretty it's well worth the effort.

- 1 **bottle (24 oz.) white grape juice**
- 3 **envelopes unflavored gelatin**
- ⅓ **cup sugar**
- 2 **cups Riesling or Gewürztraminer wine**
- 3 **tablespoons** *each* **lemon juice and orange-flavored liqueur**
  About 2 cups strawberries
  Fresh mint leaves (optional)
- 1 **can (about 16 oz.) apricot halves, drained**
  About ½ cup seedless grapes

Pour grape juice into a 2-quart pan and sprinkle with gelatin; let stand for about 5 minutes to soften. Add sugar; place over low heat and stir until gelatin and sugar are dissolved.

In a large bowl, combine wine, lemon juice, and liqueur; stir in gelatin mixture. Spoon mixture to a depth of ½ inch into a 2-quart glass bowl. Cover remaining gelatin mixture (do not refrigerate).

Arrange about 1 cup of the strawberries in a ring around bowl; garnish with mint, if desired. Refrigerate until set. Spoon additional gelatin mixture to a depth of ½ inch over berries; add a ring of apricots and, if desired, mint leaves. Refrigerate until set.

Repeat with a layer of grapes and another layer of strawberries, using all the gelatin mixture. Cover and refrigerate until set (at least 2 hours) or for up to 8 hours. Makes about 8 servings.

Per serving: 219 calories, 3 grams protein, 41 grams carbohydrates, .29 gram total fat, 0 milligram cholesterol, 12 milligrams sodium.

Layered Fruit in Wine Mold

Pretty enough to present for dessert, this salad catches sparkling summertime fruits in a flavorful gelatin.

How to Unmold a Gelatin Salad

Unmolding a pretty gelatin salad and keeping all its flutes and dimples intact can be a bit tricky for the uninitiated. Here's the best way to do it.

At least 30 minutes before serving, dip the mold nearly to its rim in hot tap water for 5 to 7 seconds. Quickly blot water from the outside of the mold and cover it with a rimmed plate (make sure it's larger than the mold). Holding the plate and mold together tightly, quickly invert both. If the salad doesn't drop out of the mold, shake it gently to loosen. Remove the mold and refrigerate the salad until ready to serve so any gelatin that has melted will firm up again. ■

Fresh Berries in Fruit Wine Gelatin

Fresh summer berries set in fruit wine sparkle through pretty wine goblets in this stunning, yet simple, dessert.

- ½ **cup cold water**
- 1 **envelope unflavored gelatin**
- ¼ **cup sugar**
- 1½ **cups fruit wine, such as pear, peach, or strawberry**
- 24 **to 32 berries, such as raspberries, boysenberries, or halved strawberries**

Pour water into a 1-quart pan and sprinkle with gelatin; let stand for about 5 minutes to soften. Add sugar; place over medium heat and stir until gelatin and sugar are dissolved. Bring to a boil and stir in wine; remove from heat.

Pour into 4 large wine goblets; skim off foam. Refrigerate until gelatin reaches the consistency of unbeaten egg whites (about 30 minutes). Fold 6 to 8 berries into each serving. Cover and refrigerate until set (at least 1 hour) or for up to 8 hours. Makes 4 servings.

Per serving: 139 calories, 2 grams protein, 19 grams carbohydrates, .12 gram total fat, 0 milligram cholesterol, 6 milligrams sodium.

Salad Dressings

A perfectly blended dressing lends the final touch to a salad, bringing all the ingredients together in a harmonious composition.

Oil-and-vinegar dressings, traditional favorites, complement many kinds of green and fruit salads. Also popular are creamy dressings made with mayonnaise; start with our homemade version and add the flavoring of your choice.

For truly dramatic results, try a nut oil, such as walnut oil, or one flavored with fresh herbs the next time you make a dressing. ■

All-purpose Vinaigrette Dressing

Dijon mustard not only flavors this classic French oil-and-vinegar dressing but also gives it body, so that it clings to every leaf of a green salad. For a more assertive taste, substitute a clove of minced or pressed garlic for the shallot.

- **1 tablespoon Dijon mustard**
- **1 tablespoon minced shallot or red onion**
- **3 tablespoons wine vinegar**
- **½ cup olive oil or salad oil**

In a small bowl, combine mustard, shallot, vinegar, and oil; mix until well blended. If made ahead, cover and refrigerate for up to 2 weeks. Shake well before serving. Makes about ¾ cup.

Per tablespoon: 82 calories, .02 gram protein, .45 gram carbohydrates, 9 grams total fat, 0 milligram cholesterol, 38 milligrams sodium.

Low-calorie Red Wine Vinaigrette

A low-calorie dressing with all the flavor of a classic vinaigrette is worth its weight in gold to anyone disappointed by bottled diet dressings.

- **1 tablespoon Dijon mustard**
- **¼ cup *each* red wine vinegar and water**
- **1 teaspoon sugar**
- **½ teaspoon coarsely ground pepper**
- **¼ cup olive oil or salad oil**

In a blender or food processor, combine mustard, vinegar, water, sugar, and pepper; whirl until blended. With motor running, slowly pour in oil, whirling until blended. If made ahead, cover and refrigerate for up to 3 days. Shake well before serving. Makes about ¾ cup.

Per tablespoon: 44 calories, 0 gram protein, .74 gram carbohydrates, 5 grams total fat, 0 milligram cholesterol, 38 milligrams sodium.

Creamy Tarragon Vinaigrette

Unlike most vinaigrette dressings, this one begins with a homemade mayonnaise that's thinned with vinegar so it will cling lightly to greens or other vegetables. To achieve the necessary texture, use an electric mixer rather than a blender or food processor, which would make the dressing stiffer.

- **1 egg**
- **1½ cups salad oil**
- **1½ teaspoons dry tarragon**
- **1 teaspoon dry mustard**
- **½ teaspoon *each* sugar and white pepper**
- **6 tablespoons white wine vinegar**
- **Salt**

In large bowl of an electric mixer, beat egg at medium-high speed. Slowly add oil in a thin, steady stream, beating until all the oil is blended. Add tarragon, dry mustard, sugar, and pepper; beat until blended. With mixer at low speed, gradually add vinegar, beating until blended. Season with salt to taste. If made ahead, cover and refrigerate for up to a week. Makes 2 cups.

Per tablespoon: 94 calories, .20 gram protein, .21 gram carbohydrates, 10 grams total fat, 9 milligrams cholesterol, 7 milligrams sodium.

Poppy Seed Dressing

One more way to celebrate the joys of fresh fruit salads is to top them with our honey-sweetened dressing.

- **⅓ cup *each* red wine vinegar and salad oil**
- **¼ cup honey**
- **4 teaspoons *each* poppy seeds and minced onion**
- **¾ teaspoon ground mace**

In a small bowl, combine vinegar, oil, honey, poppy seeds, onion, and mace. Mix until well blended. If made ahead, cover and refrigerate for up to 2 weeks. Shake well before serving. Makes about 1 cup.

Per tablespoon: 61 calories, .14 gram protein, 5 grams carbohydrates, 5 grams total fat, 0 milligram cholesterol, 1 milligram sodium.

FRESH HERBS IN OIL

Aromatically infused with fresh herbs, flavored oils bring an elegant subtlety to salads of all kinds. Even an unadorned green salad gains a new dimension when dressed with one of these seasoned oils. Or prepare Homemade Mayonnaise (page 88) with an herbed oil and let a potato or chicken salad absorb its unparalleled flavor.

Unassisted, the oil seasons fresh tomatoes to perfection. Brushed over thick slices of warm, toasted country-style bread, the oil makes a treat that Italians call *bruschetta;* it's wonderful with antipasti or a first-course salad.

For more intense flavor, choose fresh herbs rather than their dried counterparts. Suspended in the oil, fresh herbs also look handsome in a pretty decanter.

Tips for creating herbed oils. Flavor oil in small batches—1 to 3 cups only. That way, you'll be sure to use it all before the oil becomes rancid. Use bottles with small openings to reduce the exposure to air. To prolong their life, store herb-seasoned oils away from direct light.

It takes about a week for the flavor to develop, and it will increase on standing for a month or two. If the taste becomes more pronounced than you like, add more oil to dilute it.

After several weeks or months in oil, the fresh herbs will begin to cloud the oil as they decompose. Check the oil weekly; when the seasonings show signs of decay, strain the oil into another container.

Preparing fresh herbs. Rinse herbs with cool water and let them dry thoroughly on paper towels. Fresh basil is one herb that isn't recommended for flavoring salad oil; it turns black in the oil before imparting much flavor.

To add garlic, spear peeled cloves on a slender wooden skewer that's long enough to reach the top of the bottle. Then you can pull out the skewer when flavor is optimum (or if the garlic begins to deteriorate).

Herb-seasoned Oils

Below are directions for making different kinds of seasoned oils.

Dill Oil. Push, stem first, 2 or 3 large **seed heads of fresh dill** into a 1- to 3-cup narrow-necked bottle. Fill with **olive oil** (extra-virgin, if desired) or salad oil. Close tightly and let stand for at least a week before using.

Fennel Oil. Stuff 4 to 8 slender **fresh fennel stems** with feathery green leaves attached into a 1- to 3-cup narrow-necked bottle. Add 1 tablespoon lightly crushed **fennel seeds** and fill with **olive oil** (extra-virgin, if desired) or salad oil. Close tightly and let stand for at least a week before using.

Fresh Green Herbs Oil. In a 2- to 3-cup narrow-necked bottle, put 4 to 6 *each* **fresh thyme sprigs, fresh tarragon sprigs, fresh rosemary sprigs, and fresh sage sprigs;** 1 or 2 **fresh or dry bay leaves;** and 1 teaspoon **whole black peppercorns.** Fill with **olive oil** (extra-virgin, if desired) or salad oil. Close tightly and let stand for at least a week before using.

Solo Herb Oil. Follow directions for **Fresh Green Herbs Oil,** but use 4 to 6 sprigs of any *one* of the **herbs** above in a 1- to 1½-cup bottle with **olive oil** or salad oil and **whole black peppercorns.** Close tightly and let stand for at least a week before using. ▪

Herbed Salad Oils

Fresh herbs (from left: rosemary, dill, and fennel with seeds) impart eloquent flavors to oil.

Homemade Mayonnaise

Fluffy fresh mayonnaise enhances a variety of salad-makings, such as tiny Pacific shrimp and asparagus spears.

a few drops at a time at first, then increasing to a slow, steady stream about $\frac{1}{16}$ inch wide. (Add oil as slowly as possible.) Season with salt to taste, if desired.

If made ahead, cover and refrigerate for up to 2 weeks. Makes about 1½ cups.

Per tablespoon: 84 calories, .25 gram protein, .07 gram carbohydrates, 9 grams total fat, 11 milligrams cholesterol, 9 milligrams sodium.

Green Mayonnaise

Combine 8 **watercress sprigs,** 6 to 10 **spinach leaves,** and 5 **parsley sprigs;** cover with boiling water and let stand for about 5 minutes. Drain, rinse with cold water, and drain again, pressing out excess moisture. Follow directions for **Homemade Mayonnaise,** adding greens and 2 teaspoons **lemon juice** to blender (or processor fitted with metal blade) along with egg, mustard, and vinegar.

Lemon Mayonnaise

Follow directions for **Homemade Mayonnaise,** adding 2 teaspoons grated **lemon rind** to blender or processor with egg and mustard; omit vinegar and use 2 tablespoons **lemon juice.**

Tangerine Mayonnaise

Follow directions for **Homemade Mayonnaise,** adding 1 teaspoon grated **tangerine or orange peel,** 1 clove **garlic,** and ¼ teaspoon **white pepper** to blender or processor with egg and mustard. After all the oil is added and mayonnaise is thick, stir in 1 tablespoon thawed frozen **tangerine juice concentrate.**

Homemade Mayonnaise

Any recipes that call for mayonnaise will taste best if you use your own freshly made mayonnaise. The action of a blender or food processor assures success every time. Whole-egg mayonnaise is softer than that made with egg yolks; if you use egg yolks, the dressing will be thicker and the flavor richer.

The variations that follow the basic recipe offer several delicious alternatives. Green or Lemon Mayonnaise complement all kinds of seafood. Tangerine Mayonnaise adds a sophisticated note to composed salads mingling greens and fruit.

> 1 **large whole egg or 3 egg yolks**
> 1 **teaspoon Dijon mustard**
> 1 **tablespoon white wine vinegar or lemon juice**
> 1 **cup salad oil**
> **Salt (optional)**

In a blender or food processor, combine egg, mustard, and vinegar. Whirl until well blended (3 to 5 seconds). With motor running, add oil,

Pesto Mayonnaise

Italy's famous fresh basil paste transforms mayonnaise into the perfect foil for prosciutto-wrapped melon bites.

Thick Green Onion Dressing

Smooth and creamy, this low-calorie dressing lavishes assertive oniony flavor onto mixed greens, artichokes, and virtually any other vegetable—raw or blanched and chilled.

- ¼ **cup Homemade Mayonnaise (page 88) or purchased mayonnaise**
- ½ **cup coarsely chopped green onions**
- 1 **clove garlic**
- 1 **tablespoon** *each* **white wine vinegar and Dijon mustard**
- ¼ **teaspoon pepper**
- ¾ **cup sour cream**

In a blender or food processor, combine mayonnaise, onions, garlic, vinegar, mustard, and pepper. Whirl until onions are puréed. Stir in sour cream. Cover and refrigerate for at least 1 hour or up to 3 days. Makes about 1¼ cups.

Per tablespoon: 37 calories, .36 gram protein, .68 gram carbohydrates, 4 grams total fat, 6 milligrams cholesterol, 29 milligrams sodium.

Pesto Mayonnaise

First make pungent pesto sauce with fresh basil; then whirl it into a buttery mayonnaise to make a rich dip or dressing.

Pesto Sauce (recipe follows)
- ¼ **cup olive oil**
- 1 **large egg**
- 2 **tablespoons lemon juice**
- 1 **clove garlic (optional)**
- ½ **cup (¼ lb.) butter or margarine, melted**
- ¾ **cup salad oil**
  Salt (optional)
- 1 **teaspoon lemon juice (optional)**

Prepare Pesto Sauce. In a blender or food processor, combine ⅓ cup of the sauce and olive oil; whirl until smooth. Add egg, the 2 tablespoons lemon juice, and, if desired, garlic; whirl until well blended. With motor running, slowly add butter and then salad oil in a thin, steady stream. If desired, season with salt to taste and the 1 teaspoon lemon juice.

If made ahead, cover and refrigerate for up to 2 days. Makes about 2 cups.

Per tablespoon: 96 calories, .31 gram protein, .25 gram carbohydrates, 11 grams total fat, 8 milligrams cholesterol, 44 milligrams sodium.

Pesto Sauce. In a blender or food processor, combine 1 cup lightly packed **basil leaves,** ½ cup grated **Parmesan cheese,** ⅛ teaspoon **salt,** 1 large clove **garlic,** and ¼ cup **olive oil;** whirl until puréed. If made ahead, cover and refrigerate for up to a week. Makes about ⅔ cup.

Per tablespoon: 65 calories, 2 grams protein, 1 gram carbohydrates, 6 grams total fat, 3 milligrams cholesterol, 93 milligrams sodium.

FLAVORFUL NUT OILS

Aromatic oils made from walnuts, almonds, and hazelnuts (filberts) are finding their way into sophisticated salads everywhere. Made primarily in France, though other European countries produce them as well, these oils are available in fancy food markets, cookware stores, gourmet sections of supermarkets, and through food catalogs.

Nut oils are relatively expensive, but to those who relish their distinctive flavors, they're a worthwhile indulgence. In general, they're used in small amounts for flavoring.

The initial promise of an oil's flavor comes with the first whiff. Walnut oil *(huile de noix)* has the most delicate aroma and taste. The scent and flavor of toasted almonds in almond oil *(huile d'amande)* are distinct, yet fairly mild. (A limited amount of almond oil is produced in California; less aromatic than the French type, it's intended for use as a high-quality salad oil.) Hazelnut oil *(huile de noisette),* the most potent of the three, presents the full flavor and fragrance of roasted hazelnuts.

Nut oils in dressings. Walnut oil is a favorite ingredient in dressings for green salads. Use two or three parts walnut oil to one part lemon juice or wine vinegar. Almond oil is also good in such dressings. To accentuate the nutty taste of the oil, sprinkle the salad with some of the same kind of nuts as in the oil you used for the dressing.

When you make Homemade Mayonnaise (page 88), try using all or part nut oil. Let your taste be the guide—hazelnut oil, with its assertive flavor, should probably be diluted with a neutral-tasting salad oil by about three parts to one.

You can also add a splash of nut oil to purchased mayonnaise. Use 1 to 3 tablespoons of walnut or almond oil per cup, or 1 to 3 teaspoons of hazelnut oil. Delicately scented with the nutty essence, the mayonnaise is delightful with fish or cold chicken.

Keeping nut oils fresh. To preserve the pure flavors of these elegant oils, store them tightly covered in a cool place, but *not* in the refrigerator. Though light does not seem to affect their flavors, heat does. Stored carefully, the oils will remain stable and fresh tasting for many months.

Avocados with Hazelnut Oil

Toasted hazelnuts and their oil emphasize the nutlike richness of avocados. A splash of lime juice brings everything together.

> **Roasted Hazelnuts (recipe follows)**
> 2 **large ripe avocados**
> 8 **to 12 teaspoons hazelnut oil**
> 1 **or 2 large limes, quartered**
> **Watercress sprigs**

Prepare Roasted Hazelnuts; set aside.

Halve avocados lengthwise and remove pits. Place each half, cut side up, on an individual plate; spoon 2 or 3 teaspoons of the hazelnut oil into each. Garnish with 1 or 2 lime wedges, watercress, and roasted nuts. Squeeze lime onto avocado. Makes 4 servings.

Roasted Hazelnuts. Spread 18 to 24 shelled **hazelnuts** in a single layer in a shallow baking pan. Toast in a 325° oven until skins begin to split and nuts are lightly browned (10 to 20 minutes). When cool enough to handle, rub nuts between your fingers to remove skins.

Per serving: 387 calories, 4 grams protein, 14 grams carbohydrates, 38 grams total fat, 0 milligram cholesterol, 13 milligrams sodium.

Avocados with Hazelnut Oil

To dress up an avocado for dinner, add fragrant hazelnut oil, a squeeze of lime, and a garnish of roasted whole nuts.

Toasted Sesame Mayonnaise

Distinctively flavored with sesame and soy, this golden mayonnaise can be served as a dip for cold cooked asparagus spears or as a spread for roast beef sandwiches.

        2 **tablespoons sesame seeds**
        1 **cup salad oil**
        1 **large egg**
        1 **clove garlic**
        2 **tablespoons white wine vinegar**
        1 **teaspoon honey**
        1 **tablespoon soy sauce**
           Salt (optional)

Toast seeds in ¼ cup of the oil in a small frying pan over medium-low heat, stirring, until seeds are golden (3 to 5 minutes). Remove from heat, add remaining ¾ cup oil, and let come to room temperature.

In a blender or food processor, combine egg, garlic, vinegar, and honey. Whirl until well blended. With motor running, add oil mixture, a few drops at a time at first, then increasing to a slow, steady stream about ¹⁄₁₆ inch wide. Stir in soy sauce and, if desired, season with salt to taste. If made ahead, cover and refrigerate for up to 2 days. Makes about 1⅓ cups.

Per tablespoon: 102 calories, .47 gram protein, .66 gram carbohydrates, 11 grams total fat, 13 milligrams cholesterol, 67 milligrams sodium.

Creamy Blue Cheese Dressing

If you prepare this dressing with sharp-flavored genuine Roquefort cheese, you can use somewhat less of it than with other, less pungent, blue-veined cheeses.

        2 **cups sour cream**
        1 **tablespoon lemon juice**
        ½ **teaspoon Worcestershire**
        ⅛ **teaspoon liquid hot pepper seasoning**
        1 **clove garlic, minced or pressed**
        8 **ounces blue-veined cheese or 6 ounces Roquefort cheese, crumbled**
           Pepper

In a medium-size bowl, combine sour cream, lemon juice, Worcestershire, hot pepper seasoning, and garlic; mix until well blended. Stir in cheese, mashing any large pieces with a fork, until well blended. Season with pepper to taste. If made ahead, cover and refrigerate for up to 10 days. Makes about 2½ cups.

Per tablespoon: 45 calories, 2 grams protein, .67 gram carbohydrates, 4 grams total fat, 9 milligrams cholesterol, 86 milligrams sodium.

Blender Caesar-style Salad Dressing

Caesar salad owes some of its fame to the showy ritual of breaking a raw egg into it. Here's the same great flavor, from your blender.

        1 **egg**
        ½ **cup grated Parmesan cheese**
        ¼ **cup lemon juice**
        2 **cloves garlic**
        1 **teaspoon Worcestershire**
        ½ **teaspoon *each* salt and pepper**
        ½ **cup salad oil**

In a blender or food processor, combine egg, cheese, lemon juice, garlic, Worcestershire, salt, and pepper; whirl until well blended. With motor running, add oil, a few drops at a time at first, then increasing to a slow, steady stream about ¹⁄₁₆ inch wide.

Cover and refrigerate for at least 1 hour or up to 5 days. Let stand at room temperature for 15 minutes before serving. Makes about 1¼ cups.

Per tablespoon: 63 calories, 1 gram protein, .46 gram carbohydrates, 6 grams total fat, 15 milligrams cholesterol, 99 milligrams sodium.

Herbed Buttermilk Dressing

This versatile dressing can be made with fresh or dried herbs, with or without your favorite blue-veined cheese.

        1 **cup buttermilk**
        2 **tablespoons *each* chopped parsley and minced onion**

1 teaspoon *each* fresh (or ¼ teaspoon *each* dry) basil leaves, oregano leaves, rosemary, and savory leaves
1 clove garlic, minced or pressed
1 cup Homemade Mayonnaise (page 88) or purchased mayonnaise
   Salt and pepper
8 ounces blue-veined cheese, crumbled (optional)

In a medium-size bowl, combine buttermilk, parsley, onion, basil, oregano, rosemary, savory, and garlic; let stand for 5 minutes. Beat in mayonnaise; season to taste with salt and pepper. If made ahead, cover and refrigerate for up to a week. Just before serving, gently stir in cheese, if desired. Makes about 2 cups.

Per tablespoon: 46 calories, .38 gram protein, .48 gram carbohydrates, 5 grams total fat, 6 milligrams cholesterol, 17 milligrams sodium.

Sweet & Spicy French Dressing

If you prefer a sweet dressing, you'll enjoy this tangy version of the traditional vinaigrette. Use it on romaine lettuce, watercress, or spinach, or to marinate such cold cooked vegetables as beets, carrots, or green beans.

½ cup *each* sugar and cider vinegar
1 tablespoon all-purpose flour
1 teaspoon *each* salt and Worcestershire
½ cup finely chopped onion
1 clove garlic, minced or pressed
1 cup salad oil
⅓ cup catsup
1 teaspoon celery seeds

In a small pan, combine sugar, vinegar, and flour. Cook, stirring, over medium heat until bubbly and thick. Pour into a blender container and add salt, Worcestershire, onion, and garlic; whirl until smooth. With blender on lowest speed, slowly add oil in a thin, steady stream, whirling until blended.

Transfer mixture to a bowl and stir in catsup and celery seeds. If made ahead, cover and refrigerate for up to a month. Makes about 2 cups.

Per tablespoon: 78 calories, .10 gram protein, 4 grams carbohydrates, 7 grams total fat, 0 milligram cholesterol, 100 milligrams sodium.

Green Goddess Dressing

Green goddess, a longtime favorite in the West, is delicious as a dip for raw vegetables or drizzled over a green salad.

3 egg yolks
3 tablespoons white wine vinegar
⅔ cup lightly packed chopped parsley
1 can (2 oz.) anchovy fillets
6 green onions, chopped
1½ teaspoons dry tarragon
1¼ cups salad oil

In a blender or a food processor, combine egg yolks, vinegar, parsley, anchovies (with their oil), onions, and tarragon. Whirl until puréed. With motor running, add oil, a few drops at a time at first, then increasing to a slow, steady stream about ¹⁄₁₆ inch wide. If made ahead, cover and refrigerate for up to a week. Makes about 1½ cups.

Per tablespoon: 114 calories, .90 gram protein, .42 gram carbohydrates, 12 grams total fat, 35 milligrams cholesterol, 22 milligrams sodium.

Thousand Island Dressing

Popular for many years, this creamy, slightly tangy dressing is best over very crisp greens.

1 cup Homemade Mayonnaise (page 88) or purchased mayonnaise
¼ cup tomato-based chili sauce
2 teaspoons minced onion
1 tablespoon *each* minced green bell pepper and pimento
2 tablespoons sweet pickle relish
1 hard-cooked egg, finely chopped
   Salt and pepper
   Half-and-half (optional)

Mix mayonnaise, chili sauce, onion, bell pepper, pimento, pickle relish, and egg until blended. Season with salt and pepper to taste. If desired, thin with a little half-and-half. If made ahead, cover and refrigerate for up to a week. Makes about 1¾ cups.

Per tablespoon: 55 calories, .41 gram protein, 1 gram carbohydrates, 6 grams total fat, 16 milligrams cholesterol, 53 milligrams sodium.

Index

Chicken-stuffed Melon with Pomegranate (page 69) is a delightful luncheon entrée.

Sunset
Proof-of-Purchase
ISBN 0-376-02608-1

Toasted almonds and crisp cauliflower lend crunch to Spinach-Cauliflower Toss (page 12).